To Trish

with best wishes

MANIFESTATION PSYCHOLOGY

SAM PUNCH

In memory of
my Dad
Martin

ii

Contents

Preface

Manifestation Psychology is the art and science of conceiving and realising your deepest life ambitions.

Many creative, artistic individuals or potential entrepreneurial high-flyers have had their wings clipped by economic circumstances, setbacks or disappointments that have knocked their confidence.

A large number of graduates are unable to find employment based on their education, training and expertise.

Many of us have been obliged to take on mundane, unfulfilling office or factory jobs to make ends meet.

Collectively we have felt the need to sacrifice our dreams to make a living. Consequently many of us are experiencing a dull background feeling of anxiety or mild depression as we go about our daily lives.

Some of us have talents or interests that can't be shoehorned into a traditional nine to five role and so we feel under-realised.

Many are fortunate to be drawn to a specific vocation such as being a doctor, nurse, vet or lawyer. But a lot of us are left feeling directionless, wondering what to do when we grow up – long after we have supposedly grown up, or even after we have retired.

Some individuals don't know how to bring their gifts into the world or lack the confidence to express their creativity even if they are given the opportunity to do so. They are afraid that the people around them would not appreciate or understand their work and so they hide their novels or artwork or inventions away in a drawer, basement or garage.

Some people may be approaching retirement or may have just retired but would like to continue using their experience and their expertise in a different capacity.

Many of us have traded our artistic or creative ambitions for security and survival, frustrated by the huge chasm that exists between our creative or ambitious potential and the limited opportunities that are on offer.

And so this book is not about how to manifest a sports car or a mansion or a lottery win.

The true aim of this book is to help you to create opportunities for yourself as well as to conceive and manifest a goal, project, ambition or purpose that will result in fulfilment, enjoyment, psychological well-being and spiritual abundance.

It offers ways for you to work towards these ambitions while you remain in the relative security and safety of your day job, if that applies to you.

Oscar Wilde said that "Discontent is the first step in the progress of a man or a nation."

If you feel that you fall into any of the above categories, you can use your discontent as a messenger. What is it trying to tell you? Which area specifically would you like to change in your life? You can then hold that as an intention for your future.

Guidelines

The goal that you choose to manifest as you work through this book will mainly serve as an illustrative example of how the manifestation process works.

In the first part of this book, there will be some basic information about goal-setting, planning and visualisation. If you are already familiar with this information, treat it as a review.

Although the book contains some spiritual techniques and from time to time, there are quotes from the Bible to illustrate a point, this is not intended to be a religious or Christian book. (There are also quotes from a variety of non-religious sources to illustrate or emphasise points.)

Manifestation psychology is not a collection of abstract and conceptual theories. It is a practical system that can be applied to daily life to bring about achievement and fulfilling success.

Here are a couple of suggestions to help you get the most out of *Manifestation Psychology*:

You will get more out of the book if you work through the exercises and questions rather than by just reading it straight through. It is better to make notes and answer the questions in detail. If you prefer not to write anything down, you can still take time out to reflect upon your answers in your mind. If you do decide to make notes, it is a good idea to keep a journal to record your progress.

These questions, exercises and practices are designed to help release psychological blocks, generate insights and help with the process of manifestation.

Manifestation Psychology is a synthesis of many diverse fields. It has been influenced by traditional Chinese philosophy, positive psychology, transformative coaching and education, Jungian psychology, the law of attraction, integral philosophy, psychosynthesis, spirituality, the Science of Mind and the psychology of self-esteem.

This book is to be used for information and educational purposes and is not a substitute for professional medical care, counselling or psychological therapy.

Manifestation Psychology is divided into three sections.

Gate 1 (*Success Psychology*) is about conceiving, visualising, planning and putting your goal into action.

Gate 2 (*Me and My Shadow*) involves removing and releasing psychological blocks, doubts and obstacles to your goal. It is about enhancing your self-concept, self-confidence and self-esteem so that it is in harmony with your intentions and ambitions.

Gate 3 (*Manifesting Magic*) explores how you can use the gifts of your conscious and unconscious mind to activate your inner genius for the purpose of finding solutions, generating new ideas and sourcing your creativity.

We are never too young or too old to start working towards the realisation of a dream.

Our power to create and manifest lies in the present moment.

Sam Punch, London 2012

Gate 1

Success Psychology

Introduction

Success Psychology is an introduction to manifestation psychology at its most basic and practical level.

It involves uncovering our most authentic path in order to realise our true potential by fully exploring, discovering and using our unique gifts, talents and skills.

One

What's on the Menu?

One of the best ways to attain and enjoy rewarding success is to elect to do what you *love* to do rather than something that you believe that you *should* be doing.

Here are a few introductory questions which may help to source the answers within you, so that you can find your own True North: a goal that is in alignment with your authentic passions and interests - the path that is right for you.

- What would you love to do even if you weren't being paid to do it?
- What are your special gifts, skills or talents?
- Which creative activity gives you the most satisfaction and enjoyment?
- What would you do if there were no limitations or obstacles?
- In the words of Brian Tracy from his classic audio programme *The Psychology of Achievement*, "What one thing would you dare to do if you knew you could not fail?"

Your ambition(s) may lie in one of the following categories:

- Creative
- Entrepreneurial/Business
- Career
- Financial

3

- Personal Development (e.g. anger management, assertiveness skills, self-esteem, sport, new hobby, travel, quit smoking, lose weight)

Maybe you don't have a specific goal in mind as yet and your desire is to attain something more abstract – such as more happiness, abundance, prosperity or fulfilment.

In this case, think about:

(i) the sort of events, encounters or experiences that you would like to have in life which would generate these feelings of happiness, abundance, prosperity and fulfilment;

(ii) any messages or life lessons you would like to communicate, express or teach that would instil feelings of happiness, abundance, prosperity and fulfilment *in other people*;

(iii) what you would like to set up, create, design, invent, produce or establish that would help you to experience happiness, abundance, prosperity or fulfilment;

(iv) anything that you would like to give, provide, influence, promote, support or contribute to your community, to society or to the global village.

This will help you to formulate an intention or goal that is less abstract and more specific.

You may have several dreams that you wish to realise. But for the purpose of working through this book, I would encourage you to focus on one long-term goal at a time.

This may seem like a challenge, particularly if you are teeming with creative ideas and bursting with inspiration. But focusing on too many goals at once is a bit like going to a restaurant and deciding to eat every dish on the menu.

On the other hand, it could also be like going to the same restaurant, dithering over the menu and not being able to decide between any dish until the restaurant is about to close.

In the above two scenarios, you would go home from the restaurant either feeling starving hungry or bloated and overstuffed. Neither scenario is satisfying.

Curiously enough though, when you are working towards one big goal, often smaller goals tend to automatically fall into place.

When you first begin to form a new intention, vision or ambition for yourself, DON'T think about HOW you are going to accomplish the goal at the very first stage of the process.

Focusing on the "how" at this very early stage can create analysis-paralysis, overwhelm and procrastination. It can freeze your imagination, stop you from thinking outside of the box, prevent you from taking a leap of faith or even halt you from taking that all-important first step.

The act of writing down your goal or intention is one of the first steps towards converting a big intention from "pipe-dream to possibility."

Not establishing what you really want in the form of a clearly defined intention can cause confusion, misdirection, procrastination, delays and frustration.

Brian Tracy says that writing down goals acts as a motivator and an "organising principle".

It is also helpful to read your statement of intent every morning when you get up and once at night before you go to bed. This is when the unconscious mind is at its most potent - when your mind is poised like a coiled spring on the threshold between sleeping and awakening.

The unconscious mind starts strategizing to make the goal a reality by bringing us ideas, insights and intuitive guidance. You can read more about the powers of the unconscious mind in Chapters Nine and Ten.

Asking the Right Questions

We all have the solutions to our challenges and problems within us. Sometimes these answers are buried deep inside of us and sometimes they lie more easily on the surface.

It's a matter of asking ourselves the right questions so that the solutions rise to the forefront of our conscious mind.

Much of the life coaching process involves the coach asking the right questions so that the client can unearth the best choices, decisions and solutions for their individual situation. Indeed you may even wish to employ the services of a coach as you work through this book.

How the Elephant Got Its Trunk

Rudyard Kipling's story, "*The Elephant's Child*" (*Just So Stories,* 1902) is all about a young elephant with insatiable curiosity. He kept on and on asking questions of his elders even though he always ended up getting spanked for his efforts.

One day, the young elephant was rewarded for this persistent quest for knowledge by having his nose stretched by a hungry crocodile. And he became the first elephant to have a trunk.

The story features the famous poem:

I keep six honest serving-men:
(They taught me all I knew)
Their names are WHAT and WHERE and WHEN
And HOW and WHY and WHO.
I send them over land and sea,
I send them east and west;
But after they have worked for me,
I give them all a rest.

The Six Step Coaching Model

The Six Step Coaching Model was created by leading life, spirit and business coach, PaTrisha Anne Todd of Life Coach School International, and was inspired by the above poem from *The Elephant's Child.*

PaTrisha Anne Todd teaches that focusing too much on the "how" at the very start of a project can shut us down before we even begin. However focusing on the what, the why, the when, the where and the who can generate ideas and action steps which lead us to the "how". (*Life Coaching A-Z,* PaTrisha Anne Todd,1979-2003)

The Six Step Coaching model is exactly this process of asking and answering the 5 'W' questions that eventually lead you to the 'How'.

So let's take a closer look at the Six Step Coaching Model.

What?

You may have heard of setting SMART goals, particularly in relation to business management.

The SMART goal-setting process means crafting a goal that is:

Specific – A precise definite goal such as "I intend to write and publish a book about nutrition" or "I intend to start a catering business" or "I intend to become a photographer" as opposed to a vague, ambiguous abstract goal such as "I want to be happy", "I want to be rich", "I want to be famous". (Note the difference between saying, "I intend" and "I want". Which one feels more empowering?)

Measurable – Because your goal is specific, it is easy for you to measure your progress as you advance towards your ultimate destination. You will also have an idea of how long it may take and how far you will need to go to achieve this goal. You are able to set short-term targets within your long-term objective. For example, if you have a goal to write a book in six months, you can set a short-term measurable target to write two chapters a month.

Attainable – The goal you set has to be within the realms of possibility. For example, if you dream of becoming a professional actor, your ambition is more likely to be attainable if you are a drama student, or if you participate in amateur dramatics or if you are acquainted with agencies for actors. Whereas if you dream of gracing the silver screen or treading the boards but know nothing about the craft of acting, have no performing or

7

auditioning experience and know nobody in the business, then your goal is less plausible, if not impossible. In the latter case, your first steps might be to take acting classes, or get a drama coach, join an amateur dramatics society or apply for a professional drama course. A more attainable goal in this case would be to learn everything you could about the craft of acting, if that is your passion.

Relevant / **R**ealistic – The goal should be relevant to your passions and your authentic interests. You should also be able to source the energy and resources that you need so that you can carve out the time to devote to your project alongside all of your other commitments, responsibilities and obligations.

Time-Bound – You need to have enough time to complete the goal without putting pressure on yourself. But you do have a deadline. Not having a deadline can mean not having an incentive to complete the goal.

Why?

Why do you want to achieve this goal? For example, are you doing it to gain financial freedom? Are you seeking creative fulfilment? Are you hoping for emotional satisfaction? Are you thrill-seeking? Do you want more confidence? Or is your aim to get better health?

Perhaps you have altruistic reasons for wanting to achieve your goal. You may be looking to make a contribution to your community or crusading for a particular cause.

In other words, what is the reason behind the reason behind the reason for seeking this goal? What is your ultimate purpose?

The more meaning that you attach to your dream, the more productive or prolific you will be. It will also help you to keep the bigger picture in mind.

Your passion for the goal keeps you motivated and helps you to persevere through the tough times. So articulating the reasons, beneficial consequences, powerful outcomes and advantages that will come into your life when you accomplish your intended achievement will act as a motivating force that will keep you going and spur you onward.

Is your goal in alignment with your personal values and beliefs? For example, there's nothing wrong with wanting to be rich or having a goal to attain wealth, but if a part of you deeply believes that wealth is wrong or that rich people are greedy, obnoxious and generally vile, then that part of you will hold you back from getting rich results or might make you think, talk or act in ways that could sabotage your success.

If your goal is in alignment with something intangible that you truly believe in and value, then that will also spur you on towards success.

Having something to fight for is another shortcut to success. There are a couple of controversial statements attributed to Martin Luther King which underline this point: *"No one really knows why they are alive until they know what they'd die for"* and *"A man who hasn't found something he is willing to die for is not fit to live."*

While our goal may not be something we would be willing to die for, the idea of having something in your life that you feel strongly about, that you will fight for, something that lifts you up and takes you out of the daily grind, that gives you a spark, that inspires you, is a goal that will give you another reason to live.

Making a list of all the BENEFITS that the achievement of this goal will bring to your life will help you to speed up the manifestation process. The more reasons you can think of for achieving this goal, the faster things will fall into place in your external reality.

Who? To Thine Own Self, Be True

This is potentially the most complex part of the Six Step Coaching model.

In your quest to unearth the deeper purpose behind your desire to achieve this goal, you may discover that you have an ulterior motive: wanting to please somebody else such as a spouse or parent. Or you may want to achieve this goal so that you can fit in with society or keep up with the Joneses or conform to the expectations of your peer group. Perhaps your secret aim is to prove to people that have always looked down on you or underestimated you that you can be successful.

If this reason is your sole or your most dominant reason for wanting to attain this goal, then you may need to accept the possibility that this goal may not be something that you truly desire to achieve for yourself.

Exploring these questions will clarify whether this goal is something you really want or whether it is just something you believe need you must have in order to please or impress somebody else.

Who will benefit from the implementation of your goal? Is your desire to achieve this goal for yourself and the betterment of your life and other people's (such as your children or a cause)? Or is it to compensate for something that is missing from somebody else's life?

I remember hearing the story of a woman who became a doctor because during her childhood, her father was so disappointed when he discovered that her older brother did not want to follow in his footsteps. To ease her father's disappointment in that moment, she told him that she wanted to become a doctor. Her father was relieved and proud and took her at word even though she hadn't really meant it. She ended up becoming a doctor and hating it but felt that she couldn't get out of it because of the accidental pact that she made with him as a child.

Carl Jung said that the strongest influence upon a child is "the unlived life of the parents". But many adults continue to be influenced by the life (unlived or otherwise) of their parents well past their childhood. They often feel obliged to equal or better their parents' achievements or work in the same field or do work that their parents wanted to do but never got the chance to do.

If the achievement of this goal is not what you really want, then you may need to return to the drawing board and begin the brainstorming process again.

Lord Polonius, (an otherwise foolish character in the famous Shakespearean play *Hamlet*), gives his son Laertes this much-quoted piece of advice: *This above all, to thine own self be true.*

And as Steve Jobs famously said during his commencement address at Stanford University in 2005, "Your time is limited. So don't waste it living someone else's life."

Who can help you?

You will need to consider who you may need help and support from as you work towards realising your ambition.

You will also need to consider who you could model in order to achieve your goal. You could find out about people who have already achieved something similar to what you want to do and then research the steps that they took to get there. You adopt their strategy but leave out any wrong turnings or missteps they may have made along the way.

Who can you tell?

It's recommended that you don't tell anyone (including friends and family members) about your goal in the very early stages - unless it is your coach, mentor or you are a member of a "mastermind" group of like-minded people.

So why shouldn't you tell people at first?

Reason 1 - Kind, well-meaning and well-intentioned friends or family members may obligingly you give you every reason under the sun as to why your goal won't be achievable. They will encourage you to do something more realistic instead, to play it safe, and to remain within your comfort zone – and even if you do to decide to persevere with your goal, the doubts will still be seeded at the back of your mind.

Of course, there is always room for constructive criticism, realism and feedback - but just not in the early stages when you are sowing the seeds of your vision and your dream is still in embryo. Your plans may never get off the ground if you are hit with a heavy dose of criticism before you take off.

11

Reason 2 – The crabs in a bucket phenomenon or what is known as "crab mentality".

This is less well-intentioned. Some of the people around you might wish to put you off from pursuing your goal. But they are doing it from the mindset of "if I can't have it, neither can you."

If one crab is put in a bucket, it can eventually clamber out. But if there are several crabs in a bucket, none of them will get out because they will keep dragging each other down.

There is also the phenomenon of Tall Poppy Syndrome where people attempt to cut down those who are accomplishing things through talent, skill and initiative. In the political arena, it is often referred to as "the politics of envy".

On an individual level, Tall Poppy Syndrome can be competitive, aggressive, spiteful and vindictive. It is rooted in trying to keep everybody "in their place" and at the same level, miserable and going nowhere. It is a "who do you think you are?" type of mentality.

There may be people around you who want to maintain the *status quo* and who may feel threatened or abandoned by your desire to pursue something that would fulfil you, particularly if it is something bold and ambitious.

Sometimes there is also the idea that you are betraying your community or turning your back on them by seeking to change your life.

If you do find yourself experiencing these kinds of attitudes from the people around you, it is important to remember that their criticism is rarely anything directly to do with you. Their attitude is rooted within their own issues, life challenges, insecurities and hang-ups. It is important not to personalise their behaviour or view it as a direct attack against you. It is a social or psychological phenomenon that occurs in many cultural groups, particularly in the English speaking cultures of the world.

Where?

These may be simpler questions to explore and answer.

Where will your goal take place? Where will you work towards your goal? Where are you headed? Where do you need to be right now? Where do you need to be when you have completed your goal?

When?

So when are you going to work on your project? Are you going to devote your weekends to your goal or your evenings when you come home after work? How much time do you think you will need to devote to it daily, weekly or monthly?

It is as important to schedule your times of rest, renewal and rejuvenation as it is to arrange the timetable for working towards your goal. If it is an ambition that requires intellectual or academic study or physical work and you also have a full-time or part-time job and family commitments, it is all the more important to build "Time Out" into your schedule for a healthy work-life balance.

The Baseline and the Deadline

Your baseline is where you are starting out. What are the existing factors that you presently have that can move you towards your goal? What do you already know, what can you already do and what are the things that are currently missing?

It is recommended that you make a note of your baseline, that is, your current position, at the outset of your project so that you can chart your progress. You may like to date it.

It will also give you a boost as you move towards your goal. You will be able to see how much you are achieving if you clearly remember where you started out.

So it doesn't matter if you are starting from scratch, or you already have some knowledge of what you need to do. Make a written record of it and date it so that you can review your progress at regular stages and assess how slow or fast you may be working.

Setting your deadline will depend on the nature of your goal. Maybe the deadline is not something you can fix and is outside of your hands, such as an examination or competition date or an audition. But for a creative or entrepreneurial goal, perhaps the deadline is more flexible and within your control.

It is recommended that you set a deadline for yourself – even if you don't need to. This will act as a motivator and help you to avoid too much procrastination. However setting a deadline that is too soon will put you under a lot of pressure and take some of the enjoyment out of the process. If you are also working and juggling other commitments, this will just add to your stress.

If you set a deadline that is too far away, you run the risk of having too much time to think, too much time to plan and not enough impetus to start taking action.

To set a manageable deadline:

1. First imagine the ideal date by which you would like to achieve this outcome. For example, you may want to lose a certain amount of weight and you'd like to lose it in a month or sooner if possible. Write down that date.
2. Now evaluate that date. Can you realistically see yourself achieving this deadline by then? To relieve the pressure, you may want to set a secondary deadline by giving yourself an extra two to four weeks.
3. Aim to achieve your goal by your ideal date but always bear in mind that you have created an agreed extension with yourself, if other events in life occur that might temporarily interrupt your schedule.

Writing down your goal

Writer Iyanla Vanzant says that you need to set out your real intentions at the start of any endeavour to avoid disappointment.

14

So first you need to clearly articulate your intention by answering these three key questions.

1) What will you have created once you have achieved your goal? (It could be something specific [like a sculpture] or it could be something abstract like [success])

Answer: It is my intention to create _____

2) What will the achievement of this goal say about you?

Answer: Achieving this goal demonstrates that I am a

_____

3) Who else will be helped by the achievement of this goal?

Answer: [The goal]_____ has helped others by _____

Then write down your goal in the present tense as if you have already achieved it using the answers to the three above questions as a framework.

For example, *"I have written and published a novel about skydiving and it is widely read and enjoyed by millions of people. Writing this novel has helped me to **create** a sense of fulfilment, enjoyment and an extra source of income. Writing this novel **demonstrates** that I am a creative imaginative successful writer. Reading this novel has **helped others** by inspiring them to take up and experience the joys of skydiving."*

Read your statement of intent first thing in the morning when you get up and again at night before you go to bed.

After exploring the answers to all the above 'W' questions, you may realise that you have arrived at the "how" or, at the very least, you have a preliminary roadmap for the pursuit of your dream. The journey has begun.

Two

Your Roadmaps for Manifestation

As you move towards your goal, dream, project or ambition, you may find it helpful to use a kind of framework or template to keep you moving forward.

Here are two models that you can use. The first one is called the Cycle of Creativity. The second one is called the Birth Model.

The Cycle of Creativity

This roadmap is easily adaptable for all kinds of goals or projects. I call it the cycle of creativity because it is based on the Creation Cycle, a concept that comes from Traditional Chinese Medicine.

This is one of the pathways that you can follow as you work through this book.

1. Inspiration
2. Organisation
3. Self-Actualisation
4. Implementation and Action
5. Review and Release
6. Relax and Reflect

Stage 1: Inspiration

The first stage is that lightbulb flash or "Eureka!" moment when you first get your idea or receive your earliest spark of inspiration. You see and sow the seed of your dream goal.

This stage involves unconscious guidance and intuitive knowing. It encompasses the imagination, daydreams and

17

nightdreams. It is the stage when your Creative Vision emerges organically.

This is the fun part before the actual work towards your goal begins, when you can give your imagination free reign.

So once you receive your INITIAL idea, visualise your preferred END RESULT. This is the vision of the best possible outcome that you can imagine or that you are comfortable with.

Stage 2: Organisation

The saying, "If you fail to plan, you plan to fail" holds true here.

But we must also beware of planning our life away and never getting anything done. Creating a rolling plan is a way of striking a happy balance. In essence, it means planning your results in reverse order by looking at your best possible outcome and planning backwards.

This is also the stage where you do your research, gather your resources, organise your schedule, structure your path and set up your environment so that it is compatible with your work towards your goal.

You DON'T need to know all the steps beforehand. You just need to know the first step in detail and set measurable targets and short-term goals along the way.

Stage 3: Self-Actualisation

The level of your self-esteem dictates your destiny, your results and the degree of satisfaction that you attain from your results.

If your self-concept and psychological identity are in conflict with the goal that you wish to achieve, it will slow down your progress or even derail your attempts at success. You have to believe deep within yourself that you are worthy of what you intend to manifest or accomplish.

So after visualising your end result, researching and planning your work towards your goal, you then turn your attention towards your mindset.

This is the stage where you work on yourself holistically (mind, body and spirit) to make sure that your self-belief and self-image are congruent with your end vision. This is the phase of deep transformation and change.

Stage 4: Implementation

This stage represents action, creativity and productivity. It is dynamic, pro-active, pragmatic, practical and constructive. This is the phase of the execution of your goal.

Stage 5: Review and Release

You've now reached the stage where you can step back from your project and cast an impartial and detached eye in order to review your journey so far. This is also the point where you can ask for feedback from others (if applicable).

During this phase, you refine the details, evaluate your progress and adjust your goals, if necessary.

Take the time to pat yourself on the back if you have reached your targets and milestones. Celebrate your hard work even if it may not have turned out as perfect as you wished.

At this stage you are learning to detach yourself from the ultimate outcome of your efforts. You also continue to release resentments or painful memories that conflict with your goal. Releasing techniques provide one of the speediest shortcuts to manifestation. They are the most challenging but also the most rewarding part of this phase. When done effectively and routinely, positive results are sometimes instantaneous.

Stage 6: Relaxation

You need to schedule time to relax and rejuvenate yourself so that you are always working towards your goal with fresh eyes and a renewed spirit. In this way, you avoid burnout and are able to return to your work inspired and re-motivated.

The cycle of creativity, as the name suggests, is cyclical not linear. You may repeat the cycle many times as you work within the same project. You don't have to go through all the stages in the order described above but that is the easiest way to move through the cycle. If you do go through all of the stages of the process, success can become inevitable.

You will find more detailed information about each of the six stages included in the Cycle of Creativity as you progress through this book.

The Birth Model

If you have a long-term plan, creative project or business goal that you are starting from scratch, you may feel frustrated or overwhelmed at the huge gap that exists between the vision of your goal fully realised and your initial idea which may still be in its very early stages.

If you look at this journey in the following terms, it may help to ease any impatience you may be feeling about what may seem to be the painfully slow development of a project.

Stage 1: Conception

The idea is conceived. (This corresponds to the stage of inspiration in the Cycle of Creativity model).

Stage 2: Gestation

The ideas grow, percolate and develop in the womb of your mind. You may be feeling pregnant with ideas. But it is still potential rather than actual.

Stage 3: Birth

The idea becomes a physical reality. It is built, created, established or manifested (depending on the context of your particular project). But it is still new, still needs a lot of nurturing and cannot function independently.

Stage 4: Growing Pains

At some point, you may encounter teething problems, obstacles, setbacks, delays and unexpected hindrances. This is the stage where you generate solutions and battle with hitherto unforeseen situations.

Stage 5: Leaving the nest

The idea has taken on its own reality and become independent of yourself. It has become its own entity. Just as a child is composed of ingredients from both his father and mother but is still his own unique being, so too is your creation. It is part of you but it will continue to grow, develop, thrive and flourish independently of you. It may continue to encounter setbacks, obstacles, disappointments and delays but you cannot protect your child from the world. The child (your creation) has to go out into the world and encounter other people's opinions, feedback, critique, spite, praise, adulation, and you have to be a strong enough container to hold these experiences.

There are two different methods of planning that I would now like to introduce.

The first way is more suited to people who are working towards manifesting a big project that will take a specific amount of time and which may involve carrying out a lot of action steps. This method is also more suited to people who enjoy brainstorming, making to-do lists and working within an organised structure.

The second method is more suited to people whose goal might be creative, spiritual or to do with their personal development. It

21

is also a more suitable method for people who prefer to go with the flow rather than working towards completing very specific tasks within very rigid timelines.

Read each method first before you decide which one you would like to use. If you are undecided, or if your project could fit into both categories, you may like to try both methods to see which one works better for you.

The Rolling Plan

This is a short-term flexible plan that you update and adjust as you go along, a bit like a contract offered by a mobile phone provider.

The rolling plan is a really effective strategy to put into practice. It helps us to avoid the temptation of visualising what we want and then just waiting for something to happen because visualisation without action is just daydreaming.

At the other end of the spectrum, the rolling plan helps us to avoid running around in circles in a scattered fashion trying to do too much at once, burning ourselves out and getting completely overwhelmed.

This method is flexible and easily adaptable because you can move your "goalposts" within short periods of time. This helps to reduce that feeling of overwhelm, the fear of the journey or the dread of the process that it will take for you to get from where you are now to where you want to be.

The rolling plan also helps us avoid the problem of planning in too much rigorous detail and never getting anything done, or as some people put it, "planning your life away."

However it is necessary to put some kind of plan into place so that you have a clear idea of where you're going.

Before creating your plan, as part of your general organisation strategy, you are encouraged to gather research, gain knowledge and be well-informed about what you are intending to do.

When you are gathering your research, discover the people who might be able to help you as well as resources or organisations that might be able to assist you.

This is also the time to strategically plan how much time a week you'll need to devote to your goal, if you haven't worked this out already.

However don't try to know everything before you start otherwise you'll never begin. Avoid procrastination by inserting your research time into your rolling plan and setting a limit on the amount of time you allocate towards research.

The rolling plan is a six step process.

If you have worked through the exercises and questions in Chapter One, you would already have made an approximate estimate or set a comfortable deadline which would give you the time and space to manifest your goal. Therefore you can now plan your "results in reverse" as leading business coach, Lou D'Alo terms it.

For example, if your goal is going to take you an estimated 90 days to accomplish, you ask yourself, "What do I have to do in the next 90 days to make this a reality?" and you do a quick brainstorm, mindmap or list based on your research.

If your goal is intended to take you six months to achieve, you perform the same process but instead you ask yourself , "What do I have to do in the next six months to make this a reality?"

And if your goal is meant to take you a year to accomplish, you make a list, do a brainstorm or create a mindmap based on all the things that you may have to do within the next year related to this vision.

In the next stage of this process, you then work backwards, carving the time into convenient slots (say 30, 60 or 90 days) and working in reverse, you do the same brainstorming exercise until you reach the first thing you have to do in the first month or week or first day of your journey.

The easiest way to explain the Rolling Plan is to present an example.

The Six Step Process

The example below is for a goal that is intended to take 12 months to achieve. If your goal is going to take you either less or more time, you can adapt the steps below to suit your own timeframe.

N.B. Step Two will always be the TOTAL AMOUNT OF TIME you believe it will take you to achieve your goal.

Step One -Write the goal in the present tense as if it has already been accomplished.

Step Two – Briefly list ALL of the actions you MIGHT need to take within the next twelve months in order to accomplish this goal.

Step Three - List the MAIN actions you will need to have completed over the next six months in order for you to be able to accomplish your goal within the year.

Step Four - List the actions you need to take within the next three months AS A PRIORITY in order for you to be able to accomplish your goal within your deadline of a year. Your list or mindmap will now be more detailed.

Step Five - List the ONE OR TWO most important actions you will DEFINITELY need to complete within the next month in order for you to be able to accomplish your goal within the year.

Step Six – Implement and complete the action step(s) that you listed in Step Five.

Once you have carried out all the action steps that you listed in Step Five, create a new rolling plan using the six steps listed above. In your new rolling plan, Step Two will be the total amount of time you have *left remaining* within your deadline. And once again, after completing your rolling plan, you will

ONLY implement the actions that you listed in Step Five (which hopefully will now all be new actions).

In many cases, you will not need to make a completely new plan; you may simply delete or cross off what you have already accomplished or add new items to each phase of your list. It's recommended that you create your rolling plan on a computer so that you can copy, cut and paste your lists with ease.

With each phase of the rolling plan, it's important to remember that **you are only ever actively working on the actions that you listed in Step Five.**

With this method, you always keep the big picture in mind but you focus on one detail or a few steps at a time.

Sample

Please note, this is a very rough and brief example just to give you an idea of the process. It is intended to serve as a model of the Six Step process. The actual content in the lists below may not be accurate or realistic. The lists are merely serving as a template for you to create your own Six Step Process. Your plan may also be a lot more detailed depending on what you are planning to create, establish or learn.

Step One

Write the goal in the present tense as if it has already been accomplished.

I have written and published a book called: Manifestation Psychology.

Step Two

Briefly list ALL of the actions you MIGHT need to take within the next twelve months in order to accomplish this goal.

- Research the book content.

25

- Research digital publishing methods and choose one.
- Write the book.
- Publish the book.
- Create marketing campaigns.
- Set up a website to talk about the message of the book.
- Promote the book online and offline.

Step Three

List the MAIN actions you will need to have completed within the next six months in order for you to be able to accomplish your goal within the year.

- Research the book content.
- Research digital publishing methods and choose one to use.
- Write the book.
- Publish the book.

Step Four

List the actions you will need to COMPLETE within the next three months AS A PRIORITY in order for you to be able to accomplish your goal within your deadline of year.

- Research the book content.
- Research digital publishing methods and choose one.
- Start writing the book.

Step Five

List the one or two most important actions you will DEFINITELY need to COMPLETE within the next month in order for you to be able to accomplish your goal within the year.

- Research the book content
- Start writing.

Step Six

Implement and complete the actions in Step Five only.

It is often said that "a journey of a thousand miles begins with a single step".

Every time you complete the actions in Step Five, your plan is renewed and adjusted. This also helps you to incorporate new information or action steps that you didn't at first envisage or were previously unaware of. This is an ever-changing, evolving process which allows you the freedom to alter your plans but which also encourages you to focus on only one step at a time.

After you have created your first rolling plan, you may want to start a journal or a private blog (or an anonymous public blog) to chart your progress and acknowledge the small successes along the way and all the milestones you reach and the targets you hit.

Celebrate your progress along the way and remember to schedule time for rest and relaxation!

Make it a fun process and you will be amazed at your eventual success.

The Second Manifestation Planning Method - Going with the Flow

"I am enough of an artist to draw freely upon my imagination. Imagination is more important than knowledge." Albert Einstein

This may be the method for you if you dislike making "to do" lists or if your project or goal simply doesn't fit into the framework of a rolling plan.

It makes use of the mind-body connection (more information about why this works follows in Chapter 8).

This method involves experiencing your goal fully realised in your imagination and then from this point of completion

27

allowing the first step (or the next step) that you need to take to emerge fully formed in your conscious mind.

Stage 1

Relax your physical body by gently tensing and then releasing your muscles, starting with your feet and gradually moving up the body.

Stage 2

Relax the mind by visualising a peaceful neutral scene in your mind's eye such as a waterfall, or a sunset or a forest.

Stage 3

Sight - Allow a picture to form in your mind that is a symbol which represents the accomplishment of your goal.

Sound - Imagine what you will hear when you have accomplished your goal. What will people say to you or ask you?

Smell and Taste – (If applicable) - What will you smell or taste when you have accomplished your goal?

Feeling – How do you imagine you will feel when you have accomplished your goal? What sort of emotions will you experience? Attempt to generate these emotions within yourself now.

Stage 4

From this feeling of accomplishment and completion, ask your unconscious mind, "What is the first/next step that I should take to bring this vision to reality?"

Then turn your attention away from the question and return to visualising the peaceful neutral scene (Stage 2). Your unconscious mind will begin to work underground to bring you insights, ideas, answers and guidance while your conscious mind relaxes and focuses on your neutral peaceful landscape.

Stage 5

After five or ten minutes, write down any ideas, impressions, images or guidance you received about the next step of your journey.

You may receive a few ideas or you may receive a fully formed instruction for your next step. Sometimes the ideas won't come to you immediately during the exercise but may come to you later in the day or after you sleep that night. For example, when I did this exercise yesterday, I got one idea to work with but then the following morning, I found that I had received a flood of new ideas upon awakening.

Your next step is then to implement the ideas that came to you at the end of the exercise.

Once you have implemented and completed this step, you can then repeat this whole visioning sequence again in order to receive guidance about the next step that you need to take.

This is an introduction to holistic visioning which will be discussed in more detail in Chapter Twelve.

In the next chapter, we will explore the practice of holistic visualisation which is a different concept.

29

Three

Holistic Visualisation

Visualisation may seem like indulgent fantasising and a time-wasting exercise to many. After all, why should we bother to set aside time to imagine our victory when we can get down to action straight away?

It may seem counter-intuitive but visualisation tends to speed up the process of manifestation. Seeing is believing and a vision of the preferred end result acts as a magnet which can draw the necessary events, circumstances, resources and people into your path so that you can bring your goal to realisation.

When we think, our mind creates pictures and our subconscious does not differentiate between images based on reality and images that are borne of the imagination.

Visualisation stimulates further inspiration which gives us more ideas and helps to keep us motivated. Visualisation also helps us to keep our highest purpose in the forefront of our mind. Another bonus is that it can help us to change our negative programming and self-limiting beliefs.

Don't worry if you are not a visually-orientated person or find picturing images difficult. There are other ways of pre-experiencing your end result (more about this later).

Visualisation is one of the most powerful forms of THOUGHT. Thought is directed energy which has an impact on the way that we feel, act and behave.

In the movie, *The Iron Lady* (2011), a doctor asks the elderly Margaret Thatcher, "How are you feeling?"

Thatcher (as played by Meryl Streep) says something akin to, "Why must you ask about what I'm feeling? Why don't you ask about what I'm thinking? Now *that's* what I'm interested in."

The doctor then asks her what she is thinking and she replies, "Thoughts form words. Words form actions. Actions form habits. Habits form character and character forms destiny."

This, in a nutshell, is how the whole process works.

According to business coach, Eben Pagan, we are all "creatures of habit" thinking the same kind of thoughts, making the same kind of statements and doing the same kinds of things in the same manner every day.

Thoughts are intangible, but real. We cannot see the wind but can only see what the wind moves. We cannot see electricity but we can switch a light on. We cannot see love or hate as tangible objects in themselves but can only see or experience their consequences. In the same way, we cannot see thoughts but can only see or experience their effects.

In the novel *The Solitaire Mystery* (by Jostein Gaarder), one of the characters describes an exchange between a cosmonaut and a brain surgeon. The cosmonaut tells the brain surgeon that he has never seen any angels when flying in outer space. The brain surgeon replies that he has operated on many brains but has "never seen a single thought."

There have been claims from various sources (both spurious and scientific) that the average human thinks about 10,000 to 80,000 thoughts a day (depending on which source you read and what their definition of the average human is, assuming that there is such a thing as an average human).

But science has yet to uncover how thoughts really operate, where thoughts exist or where they go.

However many metaphysical teachers believe that thoughts have electromagnetic properties and are living things that produce real results.

Experts on the human brain have discovered through scanning thousands of brains that chronic negative thoughts borne of stress, anger, jealousy and so on, can actually damage the health of the brain.

Emotions are just as powerful as thoughts. A military scientific study conducted in the U.S. during 1993 demonstrated that our emotions can affect the behaviour of our cells and our DNA. Strangely enough, during the experiment, even when a person's tissue samples were taken and separated from their body, even by great distances, their emotions continued to affect and change the behaviour of their separated cells.

Thoughts are like cells. They multiply. Thoughts of a similar nature accumulate. Like thoughts congregate as birds of a feather flock together. And as every cell contains an entire set of instructions and information (or genome) to build and maintain the body, so does every thought contains the seed of your entire self-concept and your worldview.

The aim of each thought is to manifest itself.

However obviously not all the thoughts we think are manifested. Only the strongest, most repetitive thoughts survive, live and thrive.

This brings to mind the analogy of what some term "the great sperm race".

In human reproduction, 200 to 300 million sperm may enter the vagina. Only thousands out of these millions make it to the fallopian tubes. And only the strongest one out of those thousands manages to fertilise the egg which will eventually become an embryo, foetus and newborn child.

What makes a thought strong enough to survive all the barriers to "fertilisation" and "birth/manifestation"? Speed, repetition, potent emotion, belief and persistence. This applies to both positive and negative thoughts. They can give rise to both dreams and nightmares.

Consistent persistent thoughts that are infused with the strongest emotion, conviction and belief are the ones that

33

permeate, germinate and infiltrate reality resulting in the events, circumstances and conditions of your life.

Some thoughts don't manifest into reality because they conflict with other more powerful thoughts or more insidious and deeply rooted beliefs which may or may not be conscious.

Your thoughts shape how you see the world, your expectations and what you believe it is possible for you to achieve. Brian Tracy says that each human being is a living magnet. We draw into our lives all that is "in harmony" with our most dominant thoughts and beliefs. We draw into our lives events that resonate with our thoughts, beliefs and prejudices.

A feeling of stagnation and staleness in life can be caused by contradictory thoughts that create indecision and a lack of clarity.

Your reality reflects your truest and deepest thoughts and beliefs, not your casual fleeting thoughts. This is why imagining that you have won the lottery every now and then does not make it an inevitable event (particularly if winning the lottery conflicts with your hidden conflicting beliefs about luck or rich people).

It has been said many times by teachers, writers, philosophers, politicians, metaphysicians and spiritual leaders over millennia that we are the architects of our own destiny, the source of our own experiences, the captain of our ship and the author of our fate through our thoughts, expectations and beliefs.

But the paradox is that though we may be in charge of our destiny, we are not always in charge of our minds. Our thoughts are conditioned, shaped and influenced by our primary caregivers, our teachers, our peers, our colleagues, spouse, siblings and society at large. So we often have to train ourselves and learn to choose and cultivate our most advantageous thoughts.

There is, however, an important distinction to make. New Age teachers often say that we create our own reality including all the bad things that happen to us. But in my opinion, we don't create our reality in that sense. I don't believe that we attract tragedies and crimes against us or get on the wrong side of

34

Nature due to our thoughts and beliefs. These events will happen anyway as they are a part of the human experience.

However our thoughts and beliefs determine the meaning we give to the events that hit us and determine how much we personalise setbacks and how resilient we are in overcoming them. Our overall thoughts, beliefs and expectations about life will determine whether we define ourselves by the bad things that have happened to us or by the good things about life that we can appreciate right now or by the great things that might be awaiting us round the corner.

If our thoughts continuously dwell on all the things that keep going wrong, it is hard for us to notice all the things that are simultaneously going spectacularly well at the same time, until we arrive at the point where our thoughts blind us from seeing anything good or fortunate about our lives and we may then enter a downward spiral. In that sense, your thoughts create your reality...but not in the sense of creating the actual life experiences.

To reiterate, there are certain events that can't be controlled by our individual thoughts - such as global recession, war or natural disasters (these are influenced by the collective energy of the human community) – but how we respond and view these events on an individual level does have an influence on our lives, and does determine whether things get better or worse.

Therefore we must make sure that our thoughts and beliefs are in agreement with our dreams and our wishes, if we are to make them become a reality.

The bridge between what you HAVE and what you WANT is created by your thoughts. So it makes sense to turn your thinking process into a powerful ally rather than a deadly enemy.

Visualisation is one of the best ways to retrain the mind – particularly as, with the right approach, it is fun to do.

The Big Picture

There are two statements to keep in mind when embarking upon visualisation:

1) Think big at the beginning
2) Begin with the end in mind

The first statement comes from a song from the UK children's TV programme *Look and Read.* The first line of the song is "Think big, big, big at the beginning." I am taking the lyrics totally out of their original context here but the idea is to think of the biggest and best outcome (within the bounds of realism) that you can possibly imagine when visualising your goal.

When picturing your end result, as Law of Attraction speaker, Mike Dooley always says, "Leave the door open for something even bigger". Being too specific can make you inadvertently eliminate other options or bigger opportunities that may flow to you.

When you end each of your visualisation sessions, you may wish to say, "This or something better than this." This statement creates the option and the space for you to draw something even bigger into your life, should you so desire.

The second statement comes from the *Seven Habits of Highly Effective People* by Stephen Covey. Again, I am taking this statement slightly out of its original context. To "begin with the end in mind" is to visualise what you desire to achieve (not to visualise how you are going to get there). We don't visualise the "how" at this stage because when dreams manifest, they don't always manifest in the way that we think they will – synchronicity moves in mysterious ways.

Conscious Holistic Visualisation

I call this process of creative visualisation "conscious holistic visualisation" as opposed to the more intuitive process of holistic visioning which is explored in Chapter Twelve.

It is conscious because we are bringing the thinking process that takes place automatically behind the scenes to the forefront of our awareness. We are making this process conscious and purposeful, taking the reins and directing it so that it is in harmony with our goal.

It is holistic because when we visualise, we don't just picture the intended outcome with our mind's eye but we also experience it in our body. We imagine the emotions that we will feel when we achieve our result.

We imagine what we may hear, what we would be saying and what we would be thinking and how it would feel in our body, (the physical sensations as well as the emotions that we would feel.) We utilise all five senses. It is particularly important to root the emotion and the image of your success in your physical body. This is what separates holistic visualisation from ordinary daydreaming.

The mind-body connection is crucial to this process. Just as imagined fears create physiological reactions in the body or smells evoke memories or the aroma of delicious food causes us to salivate before we even start eating – so too does the visualised goal create a physiological reaction in the body which helps to serve as both a practical motivator and a spiritual magnet.

You need to imagine your achieved goal from your own perspective. You do not watch it on an imaginary movie screen. Rather, you insert yourself into the action. You don't see yourself because you are the camera. You are the director. But you are also the star of the movie. Evoke sounds, pictures, aromas, textures and little extraneous details to make your visualisation feel realistic. Experience it in 4D not on a two-dimensional screen.

You don't use the deductive intellectual analytical part of your brain to visualise – the part that likes to calculate the hows, wheres and whys. (Sometimes called the left brain). You use the creative intuitive part of your brain when visualising and visioning.

Your Visualisation Routine

It's recommended that you begin a daily practice of holistic visualisation for five to seven minutes and then for the rest of the day go about your life as normal.

Mike Dooley recommends that we don't spend longer than ten minutes at a time visualising and that we do it at least once, but not more than twice a day.

It is important to stay in the present to keep on purpose. It is just as unsatisfying to live your life in the future as it is to live it by dwelling on the past.

If you spend long periods of the day visualising, the distance between what you want to achieve and where you currently are may seem insurmountable. You may become frustrated or your mind may begin to wander.

So limit your visualisation sessions to five minutes (use a timer or alarm, if possible) and for the remainder of your day, live life in the present.

Metaphysical teacher Jane Roberts always spoke about the "power of the present moment" in her Seth books. When we visualise, we are focusing on the future and our destination. But for the rest of the day, focus on the present moment and the journey.

Energise your visualisation sessions with the emotions that you imagine you'll experience when you achieve your goal. This speeds things up.

You can also consider what will you see, hear, smell or taste (if applicable) or say and what other people will say to you. Keep it positive.

Use all your senses, particularly if you have difficulty with picturing images and colours. Engage the mind-body connection to make it a truly holistic and kinaesthetic experience.

Don't just limit your visioning to the achievement of the goal itself: Visualise your life as it will be once you have achieved your goal. Envision the way in which the achievement will affect your life as well as all the positive ramifications and consequences.

Additional Techniques

If you have difficulties picturing images with your mind's eye (or even if you don't), you may want to create a scrapbook or vision board with images from magazines and media that represent what you want.

I prefer to make a virtual scrapbook or vision board and usually cut and paste images from the internet based on the goals that I would like to achieve.

You could also turn these images into a Powerpoint slideshow.

Strangely enough, I got the idea of turning my vision board into a slideshow from watching the disturbing brainwashing montage scene in the 1974 Warren Beatty movie, *The Parallax View* and also from the opening credits of the American TV series *Homeland*.

I thought that if bombarding my psyche with disturbing and violent images really fast makes me feel disorientated, weak and a little bit ill, then filling my psyche with aspirational, inspirational, positive images should have an uplifting effect.

I later read that photographic images carry an emotional energetic resonance. So sometimes I turn my images into a slideshow in Powerpoint with sound effects.

In her books about prayer and abundance, Unity minister Catherine Ponder talks about creating a wheel of fortune filled with images or symbols based on your goals with a spiritual figure in the centre.

Photographs capture energy as well as a moment in time. When we look at photographs that capture our happiest memories, we relive those emotions. The energetic resonance of positive images can have a powerful effect on your energy levels as well as providing a boost to your visualisation practice.

You don't have to be spiritual for these principles to work.

Abundance comes to those whose beliefs, thoughts, words and deeds are in alignment with wealth and abundance whether they are spiritual or not.

In areas of life where successful manifestation is easy for you, you don't really need to define your goal clearly, visualise, make a plan and execute it step by step because your mind, words and actions are already generating these results due to your beliefs. Visualisation will help you to become even more successful in these areas.

However it's in the areas where you most feel stuck and stagnated, where nothing is happening, where you feel frustrated and where everything feels futile that these principles are designed to work. It's in relation to these areas that you have to do the "hard work" to manifest your goal.

Warning:

People who have read about the law of attraction or watched the film *The Secret* may get the wrong end of the stick and believe that all they have to do is visualise and the magic will happen. They may visualise and then simply wait for the Universe to deliver. It doesn't quite work like that. You have to collaborate. It is a co-creative process where you visualise, listen and then take action.

So in the next chapter we will look at putting your plans and your vision into action.

Four

Just Do It

While we work on holistic visualisation, instilling a sense of self-belief and developing a healthy self-concept, we must continue to take consistent action towards our goal.

It is not enough to be aware of the law of attraction at a conceptual level. It is also not enough to put careful plans into place. Having a high level of positive belief is not enough to guarantee success. Faith must be followed by action to support your intentions.

Speed of implementation is crucial especially if you are prone to procrastination. As it says in the New Testament, "Faith without works is dead." (James 2:20).

For these manifestation concepts to work successfully, you have to put them into living practice and incorporate them as a part of your daily life.

The word "action" may need some clarification in this context.

We often casually use the term "Karma", in modern parlance, to mean a consequence, something that has a boomerang effect, "what goes around, comes around" and so on. But "karma" is the Sanskrit word for "action". The root of the word *kri* means "to do" or "to make".

In the Eastern philosophies, it refers to action as part of the cycle of cause and effect, actions which bear "fruit" (*phala*) or results. Karma yoga is a form of yoga that is based on the discipline of action. Self-discipline is crucial when working towards the achievement of a goal. Thus the actions that we take form our destiny or karma.

In terms of manifestation, there are three levels of action. These three levels need to work in harmony with each other to create true and lasting success. These levels of action can be defined, for simplicity's sake, as thought, word and deed.

41

This chapter is mainly concerned with deeds. But first, let's have a quick review of the other two levels of action.

THOUGHT is action on one level. Thought gets the ball rolling and sets the wheels in motion. Everything that now exists or that has ever existed, all inventions, products and items, first existed in the imagination. Thought refers to both your intentions and your level of faith. It could be described as the most "yin" level of action. It is the impetus, the catalyst, the spark that ignites the flame.

WORD refers to the instructions that you give to your unconscious mental universe through your casual everyday speech as well as through your affirmations and positive or negative statements of declaration or intent. Words are often described as "thoughts spoken aloud." The energy of speech can either move you towards or further away from your goals.

"And the Word was made Flesh..."

We often underestimate the power of our words. Mike Dooley, the creator of *Notes from the Universe*, uses the catchphrase *thoughts become things*. But spoken words become things too.

Word is another level of energy. What you say repetitively has a perpetuating effect. Even casual or trite remarks or self-deprecating humour can coalesce at an energetic level. When statements and opinions are expressed as if they are fact and when they are uttered in a woe-is-me fashion, they are particularly powerful.

If the same kinds of negative events or results keep happening again and again in different situations, explore your words, your tone and the content of your general everyday conversation to make sure that what you habitually say doesn't conflict with your dreams and desires.

Negative chatter circulates negative energy, as does negative gossip. Bitching about other people behind their backs tends to boomerang big time, manifesting into negative events. People who love to gossip can attract negative treatment and abuse from other people from all directions, particularly in the working environment (even though most of the time, the actual people that they are gossiping about remain blissfully ignorant about what is being said about them).

You may choose to express yourself in more aspirational terms rather than joining in with negative chatter. But silence is golden. So if in doubt, say nought.

A Chef called Chris

When talking about the power of words, I am reminded of an incident that occurred in a national competition for professional chefs which is televised every year.

In the regional heats where three chefs were competing, one chef was quietly confident, focused and very positive.

The second of the three chefs felt out of his depth, nervous, shook, panicked and was self-deprecating throughout with a defeatist attitude saying things like "I'm a broken man" or "I just want to go home". Everything seemed to go wrong for him throughout the week. The third chef was complacent and didn't challenge himself.

Somehow the shaky "broken" chef managed to beat off the third complacent chef and make it into the regional final along with the quietly confident positive focused chef who had scored consistently high marks throughout the week.

On the day of the regional final, the quietly confident chef said to his fellow competitor in a light-hearted joking manner, "I like you, Chris, but I'm not going to lie to you. I hope you crash and burn!"

It was not intended maliciously and was just a joke. The only problem was – both of these two chefs were called Chris.

And guess which Chris crashed and burned himself right out of the competition? That's right. The confident one who had barely put a foot wrong up to that point. Maybe it was *karma* in the boomerang sense of the word. Or maybe it was due to the fact that the subconscious mind has no sense of humour, takes things literally and received the "crash and burn" statement as a personal instruction from the "Chris" that had uttered it.

So as stated above, if in doubt, say nought.

"I AM that I AM"

Any adjective that follows the powerful phrase "I AM" temporarily becomes part of your identity. Instead of saying, "I feel angry right now" or "I'm feeling depressed at the moment", we often lock a feeling into our identity by saying, "I *am* angry" or "I *am* depressed", thus defining our self by an emotion and blocking positive outcomes or solutions.

Observe the kind of declarations that you make that are charged with emotion. Look out for phrases such as "I can't" or "I'll try" and "but". "I should" is another limiting phrase. A mentor once told me, "Should is sh*t".

Renowned linguist expert and psychologist, Samuel Ichiye Hayakawa said, "Notice the difference between what happens when a man says to himself, *"I have failed three times"* and what happens when he says, *"I am a failure"'*.

Watch out for repetitive phrases that you use particularly if they have an emotional charge or they are connected to your physical body such as: "It makes me sick", "I can't stand it", "It breaks my heart" or "It makes me sick to my stomach". This may sound silly and superstitious but these utterances, if repeated habitually and chronically, can have the ability to manifest.

Your unconscious is rooted in your body and your body will seek to replicate what you are thinking about. As within, so without, as above, so below.

Don't try to paper over what you are feeling with a flowery affirmation if you are feeling angry or depressed. Acknowledge what you are feeling in the moment. But don't define yourself by it. This will allow the experience to pass away.

It is better to avoid voicing absolute statements, simplistic declarations or comments that derive from black-and-white thinking. These would be statements such as "Life is...", "The world is..." or "Men are..."

Any adjective that follows the verb "to be" (I am, it is, we are, you were etc.) can either empower you and expand your self-concept or lock down your self-image and shut down your options.

If you believe that something is "just the way it is", it becomes a fact and closes off other possibilities. Some people say that truth evolves and is not fixed.

Deeds

"What you do speaks so loudly, I cannot hear what you say."
Ralph Waldo Emerson

DEEDS are sometimes described as "thoughts in action". Deeds are the most "yang" level of action.

Your habits are largely unconscious. But pay attention to your repetitive behaviours and reflect on whether they are in or out of alignment with your goals. You can lie to yourself and to others through the spoken word. You may say things out loud that you don't truly believe or repeat positive affirmations that don't really resonate with you. But your repetitive behaviours and habits often correspond to your deepest and most hidden thoughts. Your habits often reveal your true levels of commitment and discipline. Often you can tell what a person really believes, not by what they say, but by what they do.

We can work backwards and change our negative beliefs by changing our behaviours rather than stopping to figure out and analyse what our negative beliefs actually are.

Develop and create habits that lead to the mindset that will get you to your goal.

It usually takes about 20 to 30 days for a new behaviour to take root and become an automatic ritual or habit. Between days 1 to 20, you need discipline, you may need to coerce yourself. Beyond 30 to 40 days, the new behaviour becomes a practice. Beyond 50 days, your new habit becomes a part of you.

When your thoughts, words and deeds are all in agreement, manifestation can happen very quickly.

Getting things done in the context of living in the real world, where you may have a job or two, family commitments and obligations can be a challenge. Maybe you are also dealing with health challenges or emotional upheavals. It is all about being able to navigate yourself through all the twists and turns of everyday life while you focus on working towards your goal.

Of course, how you manage yourself and your time very much depends on the nature of your goal: whether it is creative, entrepreneurial, domestic, spiritual, educational or related to self-improvement and personal development.

In this chapter, we will first be looking at time management and the practicalities of organising yourself around your other commitments.

We will also be looking at what business guru, Eben Pagan refers to as "inevitability thinking". This means setting up your environment or creating the physical conditions so that your sense of discipline is maximised, distraction is minimised and success is all but guaranteed.

After discussing the practical considerations of time, productivity and discipline, we'll then move on to the concept of manifestation through creativity and play.

All of these concepts play an important role in working at the peak of your potential and delivering a high level of performance.

Managing yourself, managing your time

Darren Hardy says that, "The one thing that you can never get back, that is always perishable, is time."

It's important to treat your time as if it were a precious jewel, as it really is one of your most important assets.

You can save an enormous amount of time by modelling the successful strategies of those who have already done what you are aspiring to do or who have been successful in a similar field. Make it your business to discover what the high achievers in your field are doing. Research and adopt the best practices in your aspirational area.

This is not an encouragement to be a copycat or to plagiarise. It is a recommendation to model *the way* that they are doing things, rather than to copy their actual content or material, particularly if you are involved in a creative or entrepreneurial endeavour. Put your own unique spin or twist on their methods. Tweak it, make it more efficient or streamline their process. Innovate don't imitate.

A lot of motivational/self-help teachers are talking these days about mirror neurons, or as an article in the New York Times put it, "cells that read minds".

It was discovered in 1996 that humans beings have brain cells that specialise in understanding social behaviour and the actions, emotions and intentions of others. It is believed that a consequence of this is that we become like the people that we spend most of our time with. This highlights the importance of the company we keep.

These mirror neurons are activated when an individual performs an action. The same cells are activated in the people that are watching the action being performed. This is why people can experience the same "high" or rush from watching a theatrical performance or a sporting event as the people that are actually performing in the show or participating in the sport.

Associating with or learning about people that inspire you or who are doing what you would like to do, will activate these highly specialised nerve cells in the brain and make it easier for you to model and adopt their behaviour. It is not only the children of the species that develop and learn through imitation.

Make a list of best practices in your area and adapt it to suit your lifestyle. Model what successful people did at the pinnacle of their success rather than the mistakes that they made at the beginning of their whole journey.

This is the big picture strategy for saving time.

Now let's take a look at the smaller picture: the everyday details of time management.

If you have a daytime (or indeed a night-time) job, schedule your project around your working hours (if your goal is not connected to your job). There may be a particular time of day when you are at your most alert and energised. Attempt to use this time of day for your work.

Create a visual schedule or calendar. You may have 1 to 2 hours a day to spare. Or perhaps you can allocate much more time to your project, if you work part-time or are not currently working.

As well as scheduling your project time, formally schedule your rest and relaxation/fun times into your calendar/diary. If applicable, also schedule your family time as well. Put everything into your calendar as a formal practice so that you don't neglect any areas of your life and so that you don't start to overwork without realising it.

Work psychologists claim that we are more productive if our work-life balance is in harmony and we are consistently taking adequate breaks. Your performance suffers and your morale dips without a sufficient number of breaks. Breaks contribute to a better quality of life and a higher level of performance.

At least once a week, completely switch off, maybe on a Sunday or a day when you don't have to work.

Remember that while one part of your mind is relaxing, another part of your mind can better receive inspiration and ideas and create solutions. Rest and relaxation are not only important for your health, but can actually provide you with tons of fresh ideas.

Working for longer hours doesn't necessarily result in a better performance. Work smarter, not harder by timing your breaks to coincide with the circadian rhythms of your body.

Biologically, our energy naturally starts to flag every 90 minutes or so. Most people take this as a cue to guzzle down a few cups of coffee or cans of Red Bull. Healthwise, it is better to take short breaks when your energy flags and your body will recoup by itself without the caffeine boost. Don't fight the rhythms of the body. Learn to use them. Avoid working and eating at the same time, if you can.

Working to the beat of your physical body's rhythm and taking breaks when your attention starts to wane or your energy begins to flag means that you will most probably be working in time periods of either 45, 60 or 90 minutes with a ten to fifteen minute break in between.

For maximum efficiency, devote each 45, 60 or 90 minute period to a single activity or purpose instead of multi-tasking. Use a timer in case you become too engrossed and forget to take a break.

During these periods of focused activity, don't answer the phone, read emails, Skype, update your Facebook status or browse the internet. Ignore interruptions. Whilst working on your project, you may need to make related phone calls or deal with relevant emails but allocate a separate half hour period for touching base with others.

We can't avoid stress in life. So either use it as a fuel to keep your engine going, or use it as a cue to take time out to avoid burnout.

Use stressful energy to mobilise and motivate you rather than allowing it to paralyse or suffocate you.

What levels of stress are you comfortable with? Do you enjoy working at full throttle or breakneck speed or do you prefer to work at a gentler pace? Find the level of stress that works comfortably for you and don't exceed it.

Time Saving and Productivity Increasing Strategies

Increase your focus by reducing distraction, be single-minded. Many time management experts have said that multitasking can be unproductive if your attention is scattered and divided between a few activities at once.

Don't be distracted by other ideas for different projects that may inspire you. Make a note of all your ideas as they crop up but don't pursue them straight away.

Select three priorities related to your main goal and focus on them. Put everything else on the back burner for the time being. Alternatively, depending on the size of your project, you may prefer to focus exclusively on one aspect of the project at a time.

It also helps enormously if you set up your external environment to create the outcome that you want – not only in terms of *feng shui* (a subject which is outside the scope of this book) but in terms of your project activities – for example, leaving your phone in another room, keeping your email alerts switched off, setting up your workspace to avoid distractions, moving your TV to another room if you are embarking on study or clearing space to exercise if you are going to start a new fitness regime.

You are not just setting up the environment to aid your self-discipline, but you are also creating the conditions so that your final outcome becomes more inevitable.

Just as your outer circumstances reflects your inner mental world, so too does your external environment affect your thoughts and behaviours. Sometimes you can work backwards and change your outer environment in order to improve your mood, well-being and circumstances. For example, decluttering a room that you spend a lot of time in, can help you to declutter your mind and reach clarity about an emotional, professional or creative issue.

As a bonus, if you want to, you can take this to the next level by setting up your environment as if the goal has already been accomplished. Make room in advance for that trophy or certificate. Act as if your dreams have already come true. By "acting as if", your body becomes accustomed to the feeling of success and what you embody, you can manifest.

Avoid displacement activities such as housework or "busy work" or dealing with financial issues during your periods of focused activity. Allocate a separate time for those kinds of activities.

Hours can be frittered away down the internet's labyrinth where many inadvertently become lost in a maze of youtube videos, Facebook, Twitter, forums, chatrooms and general browsing. Avoid these temptations.

Valuable hours can be lost as we sit in front of the TV. If you are an avid TV watcher, you may want to record your favourite TV programmes. On your rest day, you may decide to have a TV binge, to catch up. Replace the rest of the time you would normally use for watching TV with working towards your project.

A Spoonful of Sugar

This chapter has been focused very much on cultivating the self-discipline required to fulfil your dreams.

But whilst keeping the big picture or your destination in mind and practising speed of implementation, it is also important not to rush the process but to savour and enjoy the journey. Have fun *now* as you go along. Don't wait for that big rush of accomplishment and victory at the end. Live in the present but programme your present from the future you want to enjoy rather than the past you would like to avoid.

Creative or artistic goals sometimes cannot be shoehorned into a logical, strategic plan. These kinds of activities may depend upon inspiration and stimulation combined with your intuition and imagination (more about this in Chapter Ten).

But whether your activity is intellectual, creative, entrepreneurial or for the purpose of improving your health or well-being, the whole journey can be injected with a little creativity and playfulness.

When you love what you are doing, it is more like play than work. Maybe the ultimate aim for you is to eventually earn a living doing what you love to do. When you are doing what you love to do, you can lose all sense of time and become fully absorbed in the moment. Sometimes your mind becomes united with the work. You and the work (your art, your job, your recreation) become one.

This takes the sting out of the financial and social sacrifices that you might have to make as you work towards your goal.

This is where the flexibility of the rolling plan is a huge advantage as you are not bound to a rigid, set-in-stone, strategic plan but yet you still have a clear idea of where you are going and the immediate steps you need to take – the rest of the journey is subject to change, as life's synchronicities, events or shortcuts fall into place, courtesy of your Silent Universal Partner.

Begin to create and implement your rolling plan, if you haven't done so already. Begin where you are with what you have got, as Mike Dooley teaches. Even if your current circumstances appear to be completely out-of-tune and out-of-step with what you would like to achieve, begin to take tiny steps.

One of the abundance laws is: doing your best with what you've got before you are given more. Master where you are and you will be liberated from any stagnant situations you might be experiencing.

"The standard you use will be used for you – and you will receive more besides; anyone who has, will be given more; anyone who has not, will be deprived even of what he has." (Mark 4:24-25)

This biblical quote (though taken out of context) underlines the importance of practising abundance in thought, word and deed. It also emphasises the importance of appreciating what you have got before you can be presented with more.

So to review and integrate what we have explored in Gate One: you will be visualising your best possible outcome daily and you will have mapped out the general direction of things you need to do in your rolling plan.

Once you have outlined the main topics or to-dos, you can begin to drill down into the specific activities you need to do, connecting yourself to Universal Intelligence, asking questions and listening for guidance before you take your next step.

How you choose to connect to Universal Intelligence (be it through prayer, meditation, exercise, lucid dreams) is up to you. Methods of connecting with the wise parts of your Self will be explored in Chapter Ten and Chapter Twelve.

Use all your existing and relevant contacts. When you are participating fully in life, serendipity, happy accidents, synchronicity and fortuitous coincidences begin to happen. You might meet someone at a function or a conference who has pertinent information, who can help you personally or who can point you in the direction of somebody else who can.

Every door you knock on and every avenue that you explore, can produce something – even if it is just a learning experience.

This chapter has mainly been concerned with external methods for creating success.

As we move towards Gate Two and Gate Three, we will be focusing more on the internal methods for creating success.

Five

The Secrets of Your Success

There are three main perspectives of success.

(1) Society's collective vision of success
(2) Our personal fairytale fantasy of success
(3) Authentic success

Let's take a closer look at each of these perspectives.

Social Success

Society may define a successful person as someone who has attained considerable academic and intellectual achievements such as university degrees and postgraduate qualifications.

Other social definitions of success include being married, becoming a parent or having a six or seven figure salary.

Then there is the alpha male vision of success which includes wielding power, stepping on people's toes to get where you want to go, climbing up the ladder of hierarchy and becoming a leader.

For some, the successful are people who have careers in medicine, law or finance.

For others, success simply equals money or the acquisition of possessions. It means having the means to afford and purchase all the latest gadgets, own property and make investments.

55

To a major extent, we have been programmed into viewing these surface external trappings and symbols of success as success itself.

But people who achieve all these things: academia, the six or seven figure salary, the glittering career, the marriage and the required kids may still feel empty, unfulfilled or like failures on the inside. They may still get depressed or experience deep emotional unhappiness.

Fairytale Fantasies of Success

Your fairytale fantasy of success may be unique and personal to you. The fairytale fantasy is usually the stuff of daydreams and escapist fantasies. Often when we are daydreaming, we are attempting to transform the sometimes humdrum, mediocre nature of our life from black-and-white to glorious Technicolor through the fertile power of our imagination.

In some cases, fairytale fantasies of success remain as pure fantasy. But in a surprisingly large number of cases, these fairytale fantasies do actually come true. However, without the power of authentic success, the happiness that is brought about by a fantasy realised is usually fleeting.

Some people equate success with fame or stardom.

Many fantasise about being a singer, using a hairbrush as a fake microphone, whilst performing in front of hordes of fictitious fans. Others fantasise about being a movie star, clutching an invisible Oscar and making an imaginary victory speech. ("They *like* me!")

Some may fantasise about meeting Prince Charming or just marrying somebody rich.

For some men, the ultimate symbol of success is being able to bag a trophy wife or girlfriend to hang off their arm like an accessory.

People that audition for TV talent shows (*"it's all I ever wanted!"*) usually subscribe to the fairytale vision of success.

Our fairytale pictures of success can include images of celebrity, perhaps walking down red carpets and preening for the cameras while being cheered on by crowds of unknown people.

These images of success are just that...images. They are airbrushed pictures of reality. Behind the imagery sometimes lies tragedy. People that seem to have all the fairytale external trappings of success such as beauty, star power, wealth and adoring fans – may be suffering with all kinds of personal demons and insecurities on the inside.

This kind of success looks like success, smells like success, tastes a bit like success, but it doesn't feel like success – it is an illusion.

Authentic Success

With authentic success, you are living by the concept of the saying: "To Thine Own Self Be True".

Your life, your work, your art, your friendships and relationships are an expression and a reflection of your true self.

The root of the word satisfaction, 'satis', comes from Latin and means "enough".

Authentic success is simple and brings with it the gift of satisfaction, the feeling that what you have is enough. You pursue what makes you automatically and authentically happy and you are grateful for what you have.

You are no longer chasing the illusion and imagery of success. Your expansion, growth and development continues onwards and upwards but where you are at any given moment is where you need to be and you are okay with that.

Authentic success can also be defined by contribution and can be measured by the impact that you have on others.

When you die and lots of random people tell your loved ones little anecdotes about how much you did for them, how you inspired them and what an impact you made on them, then it can be truly said that yours was a life well-lived and that your time on Earth was a success.

Authentic success is not so much about accomplishment or the acquisition of possessions but about impact, influence and the ability to get the best out of yourself and the best out of others.

Of course, you may still get the money, the mansion, the fabulous career, the degrees, movie stardom, musical success, or whatever it is you desire – but the difference with authentic success is that you would be enjoying the experience, living in the moment and having the time of your life.

In this situation, the trappings of success are external symbols or reflections of the internal wealth and happiness that you are experiencing within.

Seven Principles of Authentic Success

There are seven core principles which lead to authentic success. These are:

1. Self-Belief
2. Commitment
3. Knowledge
4. Perseverance
5. Courage
6. Excellence
7. Enjoyment

These attributes of success can be applied towards the manifestation of your chosen goal or intention. But equally, these qualities can also be applied to any of your endeavours in daily life.

1. Self-Belief

This principle is the foundation stone upon which all the other principles rest.

To have true and lasting success, who you are *being*, how you are *behaving*, what you are *believing* as well as what you are thinking and saying must be congruent, in harmony and in alignment with your intended vision. Indeed a large part of your identity and self-concept must incorporate this vision.

In short, if you act like the embodiment of what you want to achieve, your self-belief will be unshakable. Nothing will disturb your core centre – even if you encounter setbacks, delays, disappointments and naysayers. Your self-belief will act like an internal anchor that will give you strength.

This principle isn't so much about belief in what you are doing or belief in your goal although these are important. This first attribute of success is primarily about belief in your Self.

For more information, practices and exercises relating to your self-belief, read Chapters 6 and 7.

2. Commitment

The second principle of authentic success concerns your ability to commit to your cause, project, vision or goal. It is your conscious acceptance of the challenge.

It concerns your ability to focus as well as your willingness to postpone short-term gratification for long-term satisfaction. Your goal becomes transformed into a mission.

At a more internal level, the second principle involves entering into a commitment with yourself about your life, so that you are devoted to bringing about your own highest good.

As we grow older, the realisation dawns that we will have no stunt double or stand-in. There is no time to rehearse the script of our lives. We have to act and improvise as we go along.

Nathaniel Branden, the leading expert in self-esteem, says that he usually tells his clients that nobody is coming to save them.

Once a lady replied, "But, Nathaniel, *you* came!"

And he said, "Yes...but I only came to tell you that nobody's coming to save you!"

So we have to commit to being the superhero in our own life, our own fairy godmother and our own knight in shining armour, and in doing so, we assume responsibility for our own destiny.

People who enjoy authentic success don't necessarily know how they are going to reach their destination before they embark on the journey. But they are willing to do what it takes, go where they need to go, talk to who they need to talk to and learn what they need to learn in order to manifest their goals and dreams.

3. Knowledge

The third principle of success is the willingness to continue learning and expanding your knowledge and your competency in your areas of interest.

High Performance coach, Brendon Burchard teaches that, "Experts are students first."

You continue to hone your expertise as you advance along your journey towards manifestation.

Success depends on your credibility and your credentials as well as how articulate you are about your chosen areas.

Identify gaps in your knowledge and find out where, how and who can help you to close any relevant gaps in your expertise.

Aside from the knowledge that is gained from education, specialised training and research, there is also the wisdom that we gather from life experience, from being in the trenches and from making mistakes.

Successful people are also good at following their intuition correctly or going with their gut instincts when they make decisions.

4. Perseverance

Perseverance, in this context, means devoting time and energy to practising your craft, your art or whatever it is that you want to do.

The famous example that people cite is that of the Beatles playing for over four hours every night in Hamburg before they hit the big time.

Successful people are able to persevere even if there is no concrete evidence that things will work out.

Success depends on your levels of resilience and your ability to bounce back from mistakes and setbacks. It means being willing to learn from the things that have gone wrong.

In the book *Think and Grow Rich,* author Napoleon Hill says that most people achieve their biggest success right after they have experienced their biggest failure.

Some teachers define the concept of failure simply as an outcome that you either did not expect or did not want.

One of my mentors once told me, "There's no such thing as failure! It's just another *** *expletive* *** learning experience!"

"*We learn wisdom from failure much more than from success...and probably he who never made a mistake never made a discovery.*" Samuel Smiles

5. Courage

The fifth principle of success is having the courage to be independently-minded or to break the mould. It is the courage to be a pioneer or be the "first in the family". It is about having the bravery to take risks and to make sacrifices.

People who excel at this principle know that they can't please all of the people all of the time.

Commitment is about saying 'yes' to opportunity. Courage is about knowing when to say 'no' even when you feel obliged to say 'yes' out of guilt and needing to people please.

Those who excel at the fifth principle of success have the flexibility to be able to go with the flow and the ability to adapt to uncertainty. They also have the courage to recognise when they have made a wrong turning or hit a dead end.

It is also about having the courage to stretch yourself and step outside of your comfort zone.

6. Excellence

The Sixth Principle of Authentic Success is to always do your personal best to deliver an outstanding performance.

It involves going the extra mile – if any form of service is involved – and overdelivering with the extra touches and little

61

details that surprise people. These little extras will lead them to come back to you for more of what you have to offer.

Excellence leads to positive word-of-mouth and recognition.

The excellent quality of your work, your professionalism, your integrity and your authenticity will lead to credibility, trust, recognition and reward.

7. Enjoyment

It is important to be able to enjoy the ride and savour every moment of the journey. Advancing towards your goal may be hard work but it can still be fun. There is no point in doing what you are doing if you don't like it. So one of the defining attributes of authentic success is doing what you love and loving what you do.

The Secret Behind Successful Manifestation

In order to sustain your energy as you work towards implementing your goal, there has to be a fusion between the Energy of Being (the law of attraction) and the Energy of Doing (productive and constructive action). At a deeper level, this leads not only to successful manifestation but also to a more well-balanced and healthy lifestyle.

Yin and Yang: The Ingredients of Joyful Manifestation

The concepts of Yin and Yang, as you may already know, originate from Traditional Chinese Medicine and Philosophy.

Yin and Yang are vital to each other's existence and to the core of our very existence.

There has to be a balance between Yin and Yang in nature (for example, the cycle of night and day), in our health (for example, periods of working activity and periods of rest or sleep) or in our lifestyle (i.e. work-life balance).

To manifest joyfully and with the minimum amount of stress, there must be a marriage between the energy of being and the energy of doing at every level.

Here are some of *my* interpretations of the differences between Yin and Yang in terms of the concept of Manifestation Psychology.

Yin is basically an internal energy. It is all about what is occurring on the inside. Your outer reality, the external circumstances of your life and your environment are basically a reflection of what is going on inside of you. From this perspective, you are the Source and the Centre of your Experiences. You generate your experiences from what is within you: the good, the bad and the ugly.

Yang can be said to refer to what is external and tangible. Setting goals, planning, organisation and operating from a results-oriented, ambitious or go-getting perspective falls into the category of the Yang mindset. It is all about strategizing, analysing, and list-making.

Where Yang is about going for goals, Yin is about setting intentions and where Yang is about brainstorming, Yin is about inspiration.

The energy of Yang can involve being constructive, logical, methodical, practical and doing what has already been proven to work.

The energy of Yin may include being reflective, imaginative and thinking outside of the box. Yin is about the unpredictable and the innovative. It deals with the surreal while Yang deals with the rational.

Yang is about being conscious and purposeful whereas Yin falls into the realm of the unconscious, the imagination and Genius.

Yang is about how much we consume. Yin is about how much we are nourished. It is the nurturing principle. It is about receiving whereas Yang is about getting.

Yang revolves around control and Yin revolves around influence. Yin is centred in patience. Yang is centred in perseverance.

Yang is focused on exploration, investigation and the pursuit of finding explanations and answers for all of life's questions. It is about observation, dissection and analysis. It is centred in the mastery of knowledge whereas Yin is centred in the mystery of life. Yin is at home with the unknown. Things don't need to be neatly categorised and labelled in tidy packages.

Yang is the drive for discovery. Yin is revelation, illumination and the gift of enlightenment or intuitive knowing.

In life, we are all simultaneous students and teachers through the way that we conduct ourselves and the way that we impact the people that we encounter. Yin is about what we learn and absorb. Yang is about what we teach.

Yin is about the art of listening and the power of silence. Yang is about having a voice and the power of speech.

Yin can involve partnership and collaboration with others because it is centred in relatedness. Yang is about competitive spirit.

Yin is about synergy and Yang is about synthesis.

Yang concerns the material and the financial whereas Yin is centred upon abundance.

Yin is about calling in the resources and people you need by using the law of attraction and magnetism whereas Yang is about progression, networking and moving assertively towards the resources that you may require.

Yang involves making changes whereas Yin is about generating deep transformation. Yin is about causes and Yang is about crusades. Yin's power lies in gestation and Yang's power lies in birth. Yang is about empowerment through success whereas Yin is about being the embodiment of success.

Both the energies of Yin and Yang are essentially creative. But Yin is more about conception, inception and invention and Yang is more about production.

Yang is rooted in schedules and is time-bound. Everything is temporal. Everything changes and moves in cycles. It is deadline-driven. The clock is always ticking and time marches relentlessly on. Life is short and finite. Time is our most precious asset that we can't afford to waste.

However Yin energy is centred in the present moment. Every moment is always now. It is always today. It is always this minute. Tomorrow, as one song tells us, is "always a day away" and as another song tells us, "never comes". But now is eternal and unending and the creative point of power.

Yin is about appreciating life itself while savouring the journey. On the other hand, Yang is focused on the point of it all and getting to the destination or reaching the goal and attaining the prize.

The Ballad of East and West

In everyday life, on an individual level, we may tend to identify or be more at home with one mindset, principle or paradigm than the other. For example, I do tend to identify more with the yang characteristics of planning, strategizing and organising.

When I was experiencing some health challenges related to my heart, a Chinese doctor declared that I had "too much Yang!" and that I was always in a hurry and thinking too much. I veered from being involved in too much activity to being exhausted and burnt out lying flat on a couch unable to move.

Yin and yang are energies that need to be channelled in conjunction with each other. They are supposed to complement each other and not cancel each other out. Too much yang can stifle creativity, create stress and pressure and lead to burnout. Too much yin can lead to lethargy, apathy and a lack of focus.

I have so far purposely stayed away from any gender or cultural comparisons in order to avoid reinforcing stereotypes and also to avoid inadvertently making either principle (Yin or Yang) seem more preferable to the other.

But although we may not use the terms yin and yang very often in this context, in Western society we do tend to associate men and the Western lifestyle with the more yang principles and women and Eastern cultures with the more yin ideals.

However, the differences are not as clear-cut and simplistic as all that. For example, women tend to be the multi-taskers who wear lots of different hats and who have to intensely juggle lots of different roles. This, in my opinion, is a very Yang energy.

A Tale of Two Sisters

The concept of 'being 'and the concept of 'happiness' are alien concepts to many of us – almost to the point of seeming self-indulgent and wrong.

Although I said I wasn't going to generalise, it does seem, at times, that in Western cultures, people tend to be disparaging and dismissive towards the more Yin principles. More people live outside of themselves and are disconnected from their inner reality. More people are extroverts and regard introverted or quiet people with suspicion or, at best, as if they are not having as much fun as everybody else. The idea of 'being' in itself seems lazy and unprofitable. The concept of authentic success may sometimes be at odds with the values and expectations of Western culture.

If nothing ostensible or tangible can be gotten out of it, if you can't obviously make money out of it, then it is viewed as not valuable and insubstantial – even if it is advantageous for your overall health and well-being.

There is a biblical story which (as with many stories) can be interpreted on many different levels and for the purpose of this chapter, I am choosing to interpret it as an illustration of the difference between yin and yang.

The Gospel of Luke (10: 38-42) says that in one village, Jesus was welcomed into the home of a woman called Martha. She was a good hostess who made him welcome and busied herself with serving and preparing the meal. However her sister, Mary did not help her out with the housework. She simply sat and gave their guest her full attention.

Martha was distracted and frustrated with the lack of help from her sibling and finally said to Jesus, "Aren't you bothered that Mary's leaving me to do all the work? Get her to help me." (I am paraphrasing, of course).

Jesus said (again I am paraphrasing), "Martha, chill out and stop stressing about the details. The best way of making me feel at home is by doing what Mary is doing."

Mary appeared to be doing nothing. But by giving their guest her full attention and listening to him as he spoke, she was doing all that was needed in the present moment.

If Martha didn't cook, there wouldn't be anything to eat. But if Mary didn't sit with the guest, Jesus would have been left twiddling his thumbs and feeling a bit bored and ignored.

There is as much power in stillness and attention as there is in action and implementation. Both sides of the coin are needed in the process of manifestation.

Understanding the concept of yin and yang and putting it into practice as a way of life can lead to effective and powerful manifestation results.

In this book, you will find information that relates to both the yin and yang aspects of manifestation.

In Gate Two, there will be a lot of information about your inner reality or your *psychology* because this determines your level of motivation and the way that you behave.

Manifestation is rooted in action but it also depends a great deal upon the relationship that you have with yourself. The way that you see yourself, the way you relate to other people and the way that you view reality will directly influence your action, behaviour and your results.

Gate Two

Me and My Shadow

Gate 2

Introduction

Manifestation Psychology is as much a study of what STOPS us from being able to achieve or operate at our fullest potential as it is about what it will take for us to succeed.

In *Me and my Shadow,* we will discover what blocks us, what holds us back, what causes us to self-sabotage our success and live out our self-fulfilling prophecies of underachievement.

We will learn how to confront, reduce or even eliminate these blocks to success.

Six

Belief-Ability

"I tell you, therefore, everything you ask and pray for, believe that you have it already, and it will be yours." (Mark 11:24)

Successful manifestation usually requires a firm belief in the possibility, plausibility and potential of your goal becoming a reality. You even reach the point where you unconsciously believe in it and this faith becomes as automatic a process as breathing.

There is a difference between wanting something fervently and believing something wholeheartedly. So we work on our beliefs to create our manifestations because they help to ignite emotion. (Remember that emotion plus visualisation influences our behaviour and creates consequences.)

You may find that once you start visualising as a daily practice, you may encounter some emotional resistance. All kinds of doubts, obstacles and reasons as to why your goal can't come true may spring to mind particularly if negative results are still manifesting around you as a result of yesterday's negative thoughts.

Many who teach the concept of the law of attraction state that "like attracts like". However, as relationship coach, John Gray points out, in the realm of science, "opposites attract".

Human beings are sometimes described as living magnets. As you know, every magnet has two poles (one positive and one negative). If two magnets are placed near each other and the two positive or two negative poles are turned towards each other, the magnets repel one another. But if the opposite poles of the two magnets are facing each other, they attract one another.

When you "want" something, it means you lack it (as in the rhyme: *For the want of a nail, a horse was lost*). There is an empty void, which acts like a negative pole and your strong desire for that certain something acts like a magnet to pull in the thing you want on the positive pole.

However if you want something and your yearning for it is causing you emotional pain, it is because a part of you believes that you will never attain it.

Therefore if you "want" with excitement, expectation and anticipation, your desire will act as a magnet that will pull it in. But if you want something with the fear that it will always be out of your reach, it will most likely remain out of your reach and you will always be found wanting.

The word "desire" has a different etymology than the word "want". There are two different meanings that derive from Latin. "De-sire" can be translated as 'of the father'. It can also be interpreted as *desiderare* which means "*to await what the stars shall bring*".

People who are familiar with the universal law of expectations may be afraid to explore their doubts and fears in case they become self-fulfilling results. They may be afraid to say or think anything negative in case it comes to pass. So they bury and repress their doubts and fears. But this is superficial positive thinking. Effective positive thinking has to be rooted in POSITIVE BELIEVING.

Moreover, repressing negative beliefs doesn't make them go away. They will still find a way to rise to the surface – usually as unpleasant results.

Negative beliefs have to be taken out of the cupboard and looked at in order to be dispelled. Shadows may sometimes look like monsters but they cannot hurt us – only our fear of our shadow selves and beliefs can hurt us.

Beliefs are sometimes described as assumptions or opinions about reality. Opinions turn into facts in our mind and shape our habitual thoughts, perspective and worldview. Beliefs act like a censor. They tell you what you are allowed to think so that your thoughts don't contradict your dominant perspective or mindset. This process can often make us filter out any external evidence that contradicts what we believe.

We make decisions and take action based on our beliefs. Then we interpret the results through our five senses – and this forms the basis of what we believe to be our objective reality.

TMI

It is not only your thoughts that you have to monitor, but also the information that enters your mind.

If you look at it as a chain of events: Information influences our thoughts, which forms our emotions which in turn, influences the behaviour that creates the outcome.

Information + Thoughts = Emotions

Emotions + Behaviour = Outcome

It is crucial to monitor what enters your psyche because garbage IN equals rubbish results OUT.

Where your mind focuses, your physical reality follows.

In this context, information refers to everything we absorb and digest, mentally, emotionally and spiritually - not just the factual information we may accumulate or our educational learning. Information includes everything that we observe, as well as what we absorb subliminally on the internet, through the media and advertising, newspapers, TV news and programmes, movies, music lyrics, celebrity gossip, literature and non-fiction books.

We live in an information saturated society often called the Age of Distraction. We rarely mentally switch off. Even while travelling on public transport, most of us are reading, listening to music or the radio through earpieces, texting, or fiddling with tablets or iPads. We are constantly absorbing a ton of information, some useful but most useless.

Even though we are unconsciously being influenced by thousands of advertising images a day, we can nevertheless consciously decide how to use the information that enters our sphere of experience. Choose what you are going to let into your psyche.

Remember just become someone knocks on your door, it doesn't mean you have to let them in. Just as you choose who to welcome into your home, so too must you discern what you welcome into your mind. In horror mythology, it's often said that the devil/vampire/evil entity cannot do you harm unless you invite them in.

Your mind feeds on what you consume. What you consume shapes your unconscious beliefs and this becomes your conscious focus, shaping your thoughts, informing your personal energy and creating your manifestations.

So what sort of information are you bombarding yourself with? Do you feed your brain with information that uplifts and empowers you? Or do you create mental indigestion and constipation by consuming negative information that demotivates your spirit?

To avoid negative brain programming, don't watch the news or read papers first thing in the morning or last thing at night. As mentioned already, this is because your subconscious is at its most powerful and responsive first thing in the morning and last thing at night.

We may want to be well-informed and keep abreast of current events but timing is important. Our subconscious is at its most vulnerable when we first wake up and when we are feeling tired towards the end of the day so avoid consuming negative information at these times.

The subconscious part of our mind is susceptible and open. It doesn't discern and doesn't discriminate. It records and remembers everything even if the conscious part of our mind forgets. The subconscious part of our mind is like a radio programme that is always playing in the background, feeding us our internal dialogue. Whether our internal dialogue is positive or negative depends very much on the meanings we attribute to the information that we absorb. And the way that we interpret information depends very much on our self-concept and our dominant worldview or mindset.

76

Writing or repeating aloud positive affirmations may work for some people but a more natural process is to change the mode of your constant internal dialogue or self-talk from a negative to a positive mode. A more conversational ongoing positive inner dialogue may be more effective than repeating or writing out a flowery affirmation.

Why Cell-Talk is Important

Self-talk is important because it affects cellular communication – the conversation between our cells.

In the book *The Hidden Messages in Water* by Masaru Emoto, he reveals his hypothesis that human thoughts and emotions as well as music and prayer has an effect on the molecular structure of water. The book contains photographs of water crystals next to "words of intent".

Emoto developed a process where drops of water were frozen to form unique water crystals. The crystal formations were then photographed.

Not all water forms crystals: tap water or polluted water does not form crystals whereas rainwater and water from unpolluted streams and rivers do.

However when Emoto played music around tap water, it would then make crystal formations when frozen. He used the same technique with words and phrases placing paper strips with written words under bottles of tap water. When frozen, he believed that phrases such as "thank you" or words such as "love" created beautiful crystal formations and that abusive language or insults or statements such as "I will kill you" created uglier crystals or no crystal formations at all.

Emoto's work has not yet been accepted or validated by the scientific community.

However it *has* been scientifically proven through research carried out by the US military that our emotional consciousness can affect our DNA and the behaviour of our cells.

It has also been proven that we can affect other people's behaviour and emotions through the activity of our brain cells (mirror neurons).

77

So we can therefore remain open to the idea that it is possible for human consciousness to affect water.

But what do messages in water have to do with our belief in our ability to manifest what we want?

Well, the cells in our body are mostly made up of water (65-70% depending on the function of the cell). Our cells are constantly communicating with each other. Positive words, thoughts and expressions and internal dialogue will have a positive healing effect on the water within our cells. Negative words, thoughts and expressions can have a negative or damaging effect on our cells. The importance of cellular communication cannot be over-emphasised – even outside of the context of our health and longevity – it affects our level of self-belief.

Re-Interpreting the past

The meaning you attach to negative experiences and situations is also important. It can be very empowering to reinterpret the past. You can do this by changing the mental framework from "failure and disappointment" and by asking "what can I learn from this situation?" instead of "Why did that have to happen to me?"

Reinterpreting the past doesn't mean changing the past or pretending that painful events never happened. It is not the past that we are changing but the way that we look at the past so that yesterday's disappointments no longer continues to define us or to form our identity and impact our personality. It also means incorporating your past successes into your identity and celebrating them rather than taking them for granted or dismissing them as flukes.

Nothing will make you feel successful, if success is not already a part of your identity. It doesn't matter how much you accomplish, nothing will make you feel fulfilled and satisfied if your default mode is set at, "I am a failure." You will get an anti-climatic feeling when you finally achieve what you want to achieve and be in a hurry to look for the next big thing to fill that void.

We all know examples of talented artists or stars who are at the top of their game but who are desperately unhappy, dissatisfied or insecure. They do not believe in their own success because they don't believe in themselves. As with love, the first person you have to believe in is yourself.

Pay attention to what you think: Notice any negative internal dialogue, thoughts that keep repeating themselves in relation to your goal.

The Voice of Reason

We make assumptions about why we think we can't have what we want. The assumptions are usually wrapped up in a logical, seemingly sensible, cautious disguise. Assumptions often sound like the Voice of Reason. But T. Harv Eker, author of *Secrets of the Millionaire Mind*, has said that that nothing has meaning except for the meaning that we give it.

To test assumptions, you have to bring them out, hold them up to the light and see if they are valid. Assumptions have to be re-evaluated. After all, these beliefs may have been sound at one time, but situations change as time passes and we develop. Beliefs often need to be updated so that you can be congruent when taking actions towards your goal.

Einstein said that the world's problems couldn't be solved at the same level of consciousness as they were created. Feminine Power teacher, Katherine Woodward-Thomas similarly teaches that we can't solve our personal problems from the level of consciousness where they originated.

You have to look at your problems as if you are standing outside of yourself with an impartial eye.

You have to work out whether the obstacles that you perceive are speculations or whether these obstacles are real challenges that are in need of solutions.

Earlier on, I described the 'Crabs in the Bucket' phenomenon and the well-meaning or envious people who may try to dissuade us from attempting to achieve our goal. Our own personal beliefs are often echoed in the words and advice of our well-meaning or not-so-well meaning friends. But our greatest barrier, our own worst enemy is often our self.

But why do these fears crop up?

The mind, or rather, the oldest part of our brain (often called "the reptilian brain"), is designed to protect us and keep us out of harm's way so it is ever vigilant and always on the lookout for danger or threats. The default mode of this part of the brain is defensive. It is a throwback from prehistoric times when our actual physical survival depended on it.

Unfortunately many of us still operate in this mode – but the fight-or-flight instinct is now applied to our anxieties, neuroses and insecurities rather than to the predatory animals which used to terrify our ancestors.

Many spiritual teachers have said that FEAR is an acronym for **F**alse **E**vidence **A**ppearing **R**eal.

A couple of years ago, I heard an alternative definition for the word FEAR which sums up the idea of the prehistoric fight-or-flight instinct to a tee because for many of us the only option is to run. If you excuse the vernacular, this teacher's definition of FEAR as an acronym was "**F****k **E**verything **A**nd **R**un." This demonstrates how fear can stop us from even beginning a journey.

A sense of panic can ensue just before we are about to take our first tentative steps in the direction of accomplishing something that may take an enormous amount of effort, energy or time. It can seem more comfortable to remain with the status quo and stick with what is familiar.

FEAR can stop us from making choices because we are too panicked and thinking in terms of "either/or". We think in extremes or we generalise and limit our possibilities. Freeing ourselves from paralysing anxieties means that we are able to think in terms of "I can do both this AND that".

Martin Seligman, often known as the pioneer of Positive Psychology, said that fears leads to the mode of behaviour which he called "learned helplessness".

Four Main Fears

Fear is an all-encompassing word that is often used to define our worries about what will be, what may never happen, what may not work out and anxiety about how life will change if things *do* work out.

Here are four common types of fears that relate to working towards achievement and manifestation. Identify which (if any) of these fears apply to your situation.

FEAR of SUCCESS

This may be characterised by being afraid to excel or shine in case you upset the other "crabs in the bucket". So you are tempted to continue to conform and fit in with what is expected of you.

There is also a fear of other people's perceptions about success – that you will attract jealousy or that people will think you're big-headed. "Who are you to want do such and such? Who do you think you are?" At this stage, we are vulnerable to other people's opinions, criticisms, jealousy and get talked out of working towards our goals.

This fear of success brings to mind the famous oft-quoted statement by Marianne Williamson from her book *A Return to Love*: that "our deepest fear is not that we are inadequate" but that we are "powerful beyond measure" and that there is "nothing enlightened about shrinking so that other people won't feel insecure around you."

You may have known other people who achieved great things but whose personality changed for the worse following their success. Consequently some people fear that they may become too big for their boots and develop a matching celebrity diva style ego to go with their success. But this doesn't have to

81

happen to you. It is possible to enjoy great success and still be grounded.

Success also brings with it the weight of responsibility. There is no longer a crutch. You stop having excuses and reasons to hide behind.

FEAR of SACRIFICES

Very often, to receive something big, you have to let something go. Intuitively we all know this and unconsciously we may therefore resist new opportunities because it will mean having to let go of something to achieve the goal. In this sense, the letting go process is seen as a negative loss rather than a positive release.

We may have to sacrifice huge amounts of time, energy or money to work towards our goals. And the mere thought of this may make a lot of people (excuse me once again) "**F****k **E**verything **A**nd **R**un."

There may also be the fear of a loss of identity. You may be comfortable in your old skin. Achieving your goal to you may mean changing your idea of who you are and you may be scared of losing your self-designated label or the label that others have stuck on you. Even if it may be a label that you don't like, it's familiar and comfortable. Reaching for goals often means stepping outside of your comfort zone.

If you feel stuck in life, ask yourself what are you scared of losing. Would reaching for this goal entail some kind of sacrifice?

FEAR of the JOURNEY

There is often a feeling of overwhelm and fear of all the steps that may have to be taken at the outset of any project. This can create procrastination or even stop you from starting.

The arrogance and/or ignorance of youth can sometimes result in great success.

The Houdini/Harvey Keitel character in the movie *Fairy Tale* said, "Never try to fool children. They expect nothing. Therefore they see everything."

In the same movie, the little girl Frances tells her aunt, "Grown-ups don't know how to believe."

When very young people achieve something momentous, it is sometimes because they lack the life experience to know about all the obstacles and potential setbacks or things that could have gone wrong. And so they succeed because the long list of failure possibilities is not in their headspace. So in many ways, we must be "young at heart" when working towards manifesting a goal.

FEAR of the RESULT

What if you don't like the outcome? What if it's an anti-climax? What if I get everything I want, what will I do next? How will my life change?

Fear of the outcome is also related to a fear of change and how the achievement of your goal may transform your life.

As Mr Willy Wonka (Gene Wilder) said to Charlie at the end of the movie *Mr Willy Wonka and the Chocolate Factory*, "Do you know what happened to the boy who suddenly got everything he wanted? [Dramatic pause]..." Charlie looks apprehensive. Mr Wonka concludes, "He lived happily ever after."

It may sound irrational but many of us find the idea of living happily ever after boring. Some of us thrive on the drama in our lives. Some of us equate contentment with boredom. "What would I have to worry about if everything is okay?"

Many a True Word is Spoken

Not all of our beliefs are fully visible to us because they are disguised as hard cold unchangeable facts. Sometimes, in order to uncover beliefs, we have to listen to the way that we talk. Speech is mostly automatic. Most of the time we start a sentence without knowing how we are going to complete it.

83

Speech is instantaneous. So listen to yourself. Your words may often be at odds with what you think you want to achieve.

"In the beginning was the Word: the Word was with God and the Word was God" (John 1:1)

We create through the power of word as in "Let there be Light..." and there *was* Light. (Genesis 1:3)

Words are "thoughts spoken aloud."

One of the first acts of creative manifestation is to make sure that your speech is aligned with your thought and your vision.

Sometimes our spoken words betray our true thoughts. So pay attention to what you say – this will give you an idea of your deeper beliefs or expectations. Look out, in particular, for things that you say which are in conflict with your goals.

As discussed in Chapter Four, even if your words are meant to be flippant, ironic, sarcastic and self-deprecating – many a true word is spoken in jest and this may be an indicator of what you really believe rather than what you *want* to believe and achieve.

The subconscious is always listening and it is often said that the subconscious has no sense of humour. Flippancy, self-deprecation, irony or sarcasm are not recognised by the subconscious. Saying a thing doesn't make it true. But saying it gives instructions to the unconscious. Speak and you will be obeyed...and things you say in flippancy, irony or sarcasm about yourself and your circumstances, on some level, you may unconsciously believe.

Visual Squash

Many of us have a side to our character or a subpersonality that hungers for new experiences, is impulsive, likes to take risks, wants adventure or has big plans and ambitions.

But we also have another subpersonality that is cautious, is afraid of change and that wants stability, security and safety. This subpersonality hungers for what is familiar and comfortable. These two sides to our character can cause us to remain stuck as we veer from one state of mind to the next.

We need both these sides of our character to work together – the sensible subpersonality to keep us grounded and the risk-taking subpersonality to stop our lives from getting stale. Neither side should be allowed to run rampant. If the cautious subpersonality gets overzealous, we will live our lives in fear. If the adventurous subpersonality is allowed to go wild, we will live our lives lurching from one catastrophe to the next. Both sides must be in balance.

The following visual imagery exercise adapted from NLP (neurolinguistic programming techniques) is designed to integrate these two parts of ourselves.

Hold your hands, palms upwards, in front of you.

In your left hand, think of the part of you that likes to play it safe and remain in your comfort zone, the part that wants to keep you secure and is concerned about putting money on the table, food in your mouth and a roof over your head. This is the practical sensible cautious but sometimes overly fearful part of yourself. Think of a colour, shape or texture or movement that represents this part of yourself and see it in the palm of your left hand.

In your right hand, think of the creative part of yourself, that is spontaneous, that likes to take risks, that is full of ideas, full of ambition, full of dreams and goals, the part of you that likes adventure. This is the creative, imaginative, ambitious but sometimes reckless and impulsive part of yourself. Think of a colour, shape or texture or movement that represents this part of yourself and see it in the palm of your right hand.

Draw your hands together until they are touching in a bowl or cup shape and see the two colours/textures/movements blending together, integrating, swirling around and merging so that they can work together.

Then draw both arms towards your body and to your upper chest area. Feel the energy integrating and becoming part of your body.

These two parts of yourself – Caution and Creativity, Sense and Spontaneity, Routine and Recklessness are both vital for your development, survival and well-being. But they work best in harmony together. One should not override the other.

Creative Solutions

Certain words trigger stressful reactions. Stress can shut down the parts of the brain that deal with problem solving. For many people, just hearing the word "problem" can create such a reaction. So you may also want to reframe the language that you use to define problems. You could use words like "challenge", "situation" or "opportunity for growth" instead.

Words trigger off different reactions in people. A phrase that induces stress in you may not necessarily induce stress in your friend or brother. Find a word for your challenges that doesn't have a negative emotional charge for you.

Another way to reduce overwhelm is to clearly describe a challenging "situation" in writing. Sometimes it looks less overwhelming when put to paper. Focus on potential solutions when looking at a "situation".

The Antidotes to Negativity

Answer the quiz below for further insights into your thought and belief process in order to evolve and surmount any self-limiting beliefs.

Past disappointments

"We must accept finite disappointment but never lose infinite hope." (Martin Luther King Jr)

We have to increase our levels of resilience in order to bounce back from past disappointments, setbacks and perceived failures.

Use the wisdom of hindsight to make today and tomorrow different from yesterday.

a) What related past disappointments / previous "failures" have you already had in the area of this goal?

b) What positive lessons did you learn from this disappointment or failure?

c) How can you use these lessons to empower you? What can you do differently this time round?

d) Which attitudes, behaviours, people, or activities do you need to let go of?

e) What (new) habits do you need to cultivate?

Moving Forward

a) What actual evidence is there that this goal can become a reality? What are the factors that make it a possibility? Who are the pioneers or role models? Who else has done what you would like to do starting from the same circumstances?

b) Write a statement about how successful you have been from the vantage point of having completed the goal: the reasons why you found it so easy to achieve the goal.

c) Write a "pretend" letter to a friend about your success. Instead of building a case as to why it won't work (future), build a case to say why it DID work expressed in past terms as if it has already happened.

If you have answered all the questions above, you have gone some way into exploring your conscious beliefs and blocks about manifesting what you desire.

But what about the beliefs we have that we aren't consciously aware of? As Carl Jung said, "That which we do not bring to consciousness appears in our life as fate."

Therefore in the following chapter, we will explore hidden beliefs by looking at your self-image and identity as it relates to the goal that you wish to achieve.

Seven

Who do you THINK you are?

Successful and speedy manifestation depends on having a healthy self-concept and a sense of identity that is aligned with the goals that you wish to achieve.

Business expert Brendon Burchard says that, "Who and what you <u>think you are</u> dictates almost everything in your life."

Nathaniel Branden, one of the foremost therapists in the field of self-esteem, says that the way that we feel about ourselves affects every aspect of our experience and that our self-concept is our "destiny."

We have to evolve our self-image and raise the level of our self-esteem so that it is congruent with all the creativity, abundance and good fortune that we wish to produce in our lives.

Many teachers, coaches or therapists advocate the use of empowering affirmations to help instil a sense of positivity. However, in many cases, repeating or writing affirmations may only serve to paper over the cracks in our self-esteem and self-belief without getting at the roots of the matter.

Three Keys to Achievement

The three keys to achievement lie in:

1) Our innate talents, the gifts we were born with, the skills that come naturally to us
2) Acquiring specialised knowledge, expertise and competence or training in the areas where we want to succeed

89

3) Our attitude and mindset

However there is a saying that "if knowledge was all it took to be successful, then every librarian would be rich."

Our attitude and mindset is the most important of these three keys to achievement. You can acquire specialised knowledge and new skills through training – but if your attitude and mindset is not set to one of success, you will just keep jumping through hoops to no avail and wondering why certificate after certificate does not bring you any success.

Darren Hardy, the chief of *Success* magazine, believes that 80-90% of success can be attributed to having a "champion's" attitude with the remaining percentage due to our innate talents and specialised knowledge, education and training.

With all three key pillars in place, success becomes inevitable. So be clear in your mind about what your gifts and talents are and work to strengthen them through practice or training. We need to work towards developing the mindset of a champion – even if our outer circumstances are not yet reflecting this reality.

As mentioned in Chapter Six, nothing outside of yourself and nothing you achieve will make you feel good about yourself, if you do not already like or appreciate yourself. You will always be searching for approval, appreciation and applause from others – like an elusive pill that can cure all ills.

It is possible to achieve great things whilst bearing the burden of a low level of self-esteem, but the victory of a goal achieved doesn't taste quite as sweet. Plus if your self-concept is lower than your aspirations, you may have great difficulty in fulfilling your goals because you aren't yet able to see yourself as the kind of person that can accomplish them.

We create our own glass ceiling. As Nathaniel Branden says in his self-esteem audio programs, we tell ourselves, "I will rise just as high as my self-concept will accommodate and then I will stop".

Brian Tracy says that we always perform and behave consistently with our "basic self-concept" and never perform higher than that.

T. Harv Eker, author of *Secrets of the Millionaire Mind,* calls it our "set point". This can refer to your level of income, your career, the kind of home you live in, the qualifications you have and so on.

Your self-concept affects the level of the goals you set. Though you may be capable of accomplishing extraordinary things, you may limit yourself in accordance with your ideas about yourself.

Branden describes our self-concept as an "internal governor or thermostat". Alarm bells start to ring and anxiety may set in when the potential for progressing further in life begins to present itself. Self-sabotage can take place to return things back to their natural order. Events may seem to conspire against you until you end up back where you believe you truly belong with what you unconsciously believe you truly deserve. This is not due to a lack of ability or talent but to a lack of self-belief.

For lasting success, we need to expand our self-concept so that we can welcome in greater levels of achievement and feel comfortable in our own skin and at ease with the label of "success".

You have to build into your identity the belief that you are, for example, a writer if you want to write, an artist, if you want to paint, a musician, if you want to compose and so on. Your identity has to be incorporated into your intended end result.

So how do you define yourself? Do you think of yourself primarily as an administrator, a parent, a spouse, an executive, a manual worker, unemployed or a retiree?

What is the first label that you stick on yourself? Can you add another label that is in line with your intended goal?

Does your self-concept support your dream? Can you be more flexible and make room for the other sides of your personality?

Once again, examine your negative self-talk and your internal dialogue. Do you say things like: "I'm not the type of person to…" or "Who am I to…" "How on earth can I…"

Exploring our self-concept becomes crucial if we are feeling stuck, having trouble getting plans off the ground or having difficulties seeing things through to completion.

The raw ingredients that blend into the creation of our self-concept include ideas, thoughts, experiences, memories and images about our self and about our past. These are like jigsaw puzzle pieces that make up a picture of the person that we believe ourselves to be. But sometimes the jigsaw pieces don't quite fit together and we develop a skewed or distorted vision of who we are.

In the previous chapter, I mentioned subpersonalities. Subpersonalities are like miniature self-concepts or ideas that we have about all the roles that we play in life: sibling, spouse, son/daughter, colleague, boss, parent, friend, cousin, employee and so on.

Miniature self-concepts can include our opinions or perceptions about our skills, strengths, weaknesses, talents, attributes or appearance.

One person can behave completely differently and show a contrasting side to their personality depending on what they are doing or who they are with. For example, a manager could be cantankerous and overbearing in the workplace and yet patient and endearing with his four year old son.

These miniature concepts or subpersonalities contribute to how we think and feel about ourselves. They are a memory bank from which we draw our sense of self-approval or disapproval. Whether we approve or disapprove of ourselves affects whether we believe in our right to expect happiness and fulfilment.

Our perception of our self then determines how we act and the way that we respond and react to life's events. This affects the overall outcome and provides us with the evidence that validates our internal belief. The question is, do you believe what you see or do you *see* what you *already* believe?

Sometimes we develop a mythology about our past based on our perception of our identity. We then view these myths as historical facts rather than psychological viewpoints.

Our self-concept can be described as being made up of three different parts:

Superstar

The aspirational self – this is the vision of the person that we would like to be. The superstar self is based upon people that we admire and would like to emulate such as spiritual leaders, creative artists in our field, successful people in our profession, celebrities or iconic figures. This aspirational self is also based on the attributes and qualities that we wished we possessed such as compassion, patience, generosity, confidence, empathy, wit, humour or resilience.

The superstar self provides a guide to our true aspirations.

The aspirational self may be too perfect to be realistic. But that which we admire and aspire to already lies dormant within us ready to be awakened.

Man in the Mirror

The self in the internal mirror: this is the current image that we have of our self. It is our real opinion of our character, personality and appearance. The reflection that we see in our internal mirror has an enormous influence over the way that we behave.

Sometimes the disparity between the superstar self and the self in the internal mirror can seem too huge, creating a sense of overwhelm, defeat or depression.

And sometimes the self that we see in the internal mirror is not an accurate representation of reality. An extreme version of this is a thin teenager who may feel fat or see a distorted overweight reflection of herself in a mirror.

To create powerful changes in your behaviour and performance, change the picture of yourself in your internal mirror to one that is in accordance with your goals. (This image doesn't have to be as grandiose as your aspirational superstar self.)

Because you're worth it

Self-esteem: this is basically how much you like what you see in your internal mirror, as well as how much you nurture yourself. The way that you feel you deserve to be treated often determines what you think of as your "lot in life". This influences how successful you feel and how well you perform in different areas. Events and circumstances reflect your relationship with yourself or what you believe it is possible for you to have.

If you feel competent at what you do, recognise your right to be happy, feel comfortable standing up for your rights and your needs, and feel excited and enthusiastic about going for goals, then you fortunately have a very healthy level of self-esteem.

We explored a lot about fears in Chapter Six. Fears can gnaw away at our self-esteem. Moreover, guilt about past mistakes can make us disapprove of or dislike our self.

Self-doubt about your competence and general worries about whether or not you are good enough can further serve to hamper your level of self-esteem creating stressful reactions whenever you meet with challenge and adversity.

False confidence, pretentious or arrogant behaviour or a know-it-all pompous attitude are all signs of a low self-esteem as well as the more obvious symptoms on the other end of the spectrum such as self-consciousness, shyness and lack of confidence.

The good news is that your self-image and self-concept can be changed. They are a composite of all your habits. This was the way you learnt how to be in order to survive. But many of these coping mechanisms are now outdated and no longer needed. You can learn new habits, new behaviours and consciously choose new thoughts to override the old unconscious patterns.

The best way to release the power of habitual negative thoughts, feelings and behaviours is to make the reasons for their existence conscious. Often the mere act of observing a pattern is enough to dissolve it.

Consciously reset, upgrade and evolve your concept of your identity so that it is in tune with your future goal.

We need to evolve our self-image and self-esteem – not just for the purpose of attaining the goal – but for our overall psychological well-being and happiness.

Do you know where you're going to?

We tend to identify ourselves by looking at what happened to us in the past rather than by defining ourselves according to where we want to go and who we want to be.

We need to look at the vision of what we want to achieve and define what sort of person would achieve that. And then we operate and behave through the focus of what we want to manifest in the future rather than what has happened to us in the past (if our pictures of the past don't support our future vision).

To get where you need to go, what kind of person do you think you need to be?

Is this an assumption or is this something you really need to learn, change, think, do etc.?

Make decisions based on the future you want to create rather than the past you want to avoid.

As motivational speaker, Tony Robbins always says, "The past doesn't equal the future."

Answer the two following questions to determine your strengths and your vision.

(i) What skills, qualities, resources and attributes do you already have which can move you towards the manifestation of this goal?

95

(ii) What will you be "experiencing and feeling" just after you have manifested this goal?

I think therefore I am

What you think you are deep down inside yourself, you eventually become.

It doesn't matter <u>what</u> you believe about yourself. All that matters is <u>that</u> you believe it.

Whether your beliefs are valid or not is not the issue, your deeper beliefs and expectations become projections that are duplicated in your reality.

This is why Nathaniel Branden says that, "Of all the judgements you pass, none is important as the judgement you pass upon yourself"

But where do these self-judgements come from if they are formed unconsciously?

Biologists say that "80% of what goes into generating our inner experience of the world comes from information that already exists in our brain and only 20% through the external senses". Most of this information ruling our inner mental experience was established during childhood and prepubescence.

So where did *that* information come from?

The Truth is Out There

Our thought patterns, habits and behaviours are taking us on a journey that may be different from where we intend to go.

Repetitive and automatic thoughts, feelings and behaviours originate from unconscious sources.

We are usually frustrated and confused by the repetitive and addictive nature of these negative feelings and have no idea why we keep thinking, doing and feeling what we do in spite of our willingness to change.

Often the reasons why we think the same thoughts, get triggered by the same negative feelings or perform the same habitual actions seem invisible to us. This is because these patterns originated early in life and were influenced by our primary caregivers or authority figures in our formative years.

This is reminiscent of the famous old Jesuit saying: "Give me a child until the age of seven and I will give you the man."

Small children can form simplistic conclusions about themselves from the way that they are treated by the adults that are in charge of them and these conclusions become deeply rooted emotional beliefs. Even when we become adults, we may continue to think and behave through the focus of these black-and-white beliefs.

During childhood, the front part of the brain is still developing. So if a child does something wrong and is told that they have done something wrong, depending on the manner that they have been told, the child would be unable to separate what he did from his identity. He would therefore conclude that *he* is wrong or bad.

Similarly, if a child is told that what she did is not good enough, depending on the manner that she had been told this, she may become unable to separate what she did from who she is and would conclude that *she* is not good enough. We may carry this belief onto adulthood if it happens too many times.

Part of our identity is unconsciously composed of the sum total of everything we have ever thought and believed. But a lot of our self-concept is formed through what we think we see in other people's eyes. The reflection that we cast in other people's eyes may or may not be valid but we often internalise it as if it were true and it then becomes a part of our personality and identity.

Therefore much of our identity is unconsciously moulded, fashioned and conditioned by other people such as our parents, teachers, peers, bosses and other authority figures - unless we *consciously* create our own self-concept and choose the kind of person that we want to be.

Most of the beliefs that you have, you weren't born with (unless you inherited them from an ancestor or brought them with you from a previous lifetime, but that's a whole other discussion outside the scope of this book).

Most of the beliefs that you have were adopted, inherited or learnt.

The criticism and negative feedback or comments that we receive from others during adulthood are often the disquieting echoes of our own internal dialogue.

The child you once were, you always carry with you. When talking negatively to yourself, the part that it impacts is that inner child. When you berate or insult yourself, call yourself stupid, imagine that you are saying it to your innocent five year old self and you may be able to stop doing it.

We see ourselves through the reflection in other people's eyes – especially in our formative years and we carry this image into adulthood. This becomes the image that we see in our own internal mirror. But often who we think we are, is who *everybody else* thinks we are and we behave according to other people's perception of ourselves. It's a kind of chicken-and-egg situation.

The tagline for the science fiction TV series *The X Files* was: "The truth is out there." In a manner of speaking, the truth "out there" is only a reflection of the belief "in here".

And according to some Buddhist philosophers: There is no one else out there.

The Hand that Rock the Cradle

"Do not believe in anything simply because you have heard it. Do not believe in anything simply because it is spoken and rumoured by many. Do not believe in anything simply because it is found written in your religious books. Do not believe in anything merely on the authority of your teachers and elders. Do not believe in traditions because they have been handed down for many generations. But after observation and analysis, when you find that anything agrees with reason and is conducive to the good and benefit of one and all, then accept it and live up to it." Buddha

When I use the word "parents" in this context, I use it as an umbrella term to describe your primary caregivers, meaning the adults that were mainly responsible for your upbringing. This may include step-parents, foster parents, adoptive parents, grandparents, older siblings, godparents or other family members and guardians.

Our identity is not only shaped by how our parents perceived us. Our identity also incorporates what our parents valued, believed and expected socially, culturally, religiously, politically and economically. During infancy and childhood, we are literally spoonfed our beliefs.

You may have accepted or rejected their ideals. You may have questioned what they believed or developed your own opinions which may or not have conformed with their values.

Whether you accepted or rejected their ideals, ambitions or opinions, part of your identity is shaped by how you reacted to their worldview.

Leaving home and flying the nest may take place physically but may never take place psychologically. Leaving your old self behind, leaving behind your old view of yourself can be quite a wrench. Your old identity may cling on for dear life to the comfort zone which has taken the place of the parental home.

To psychologically leave home and attain true independence may mean privately challenging (just for yourself) the values, principles, customs, rules (spoken and unspoken) of those around you (family, friends, colleagues) that you may have automatically and unconditionally accepted but which conflict with the kind of goals you wish to achieve or the kind of lifestyle that you want to lead.

This may feel like breaking the rules, going against your community or betraying your loved ones. Part of you may wish to remain loyal. Human beings are generally clannish by nature and this wish to remain loyal is a natural part of the human experience.

You will decide for yourself whether it is the misplaced loyalty of childhood confusion which has carried through to adulthood or whether these are ideals and values that are truly yours and

99

that you wish to hold on to in spite of any seeming conflict there might be with your life's ambitions and goals.

Answering the following questions may serve to guide you through this process of exploration. <u>Always remember to answer the questions in relation to your intended goal.</u>

Are there any second-hand personal or social beliefs that have been handed to you by your family of origin *that conflicts with your goal*?

Do you have any specific habitual thoughts *about yourself* which echo the attitudes of your primary caregivers (both positive and negative)?

Are there any phrases about yourself that you use which reflect the attitudes of your primary caregivers (both positive and negative)?

Do you have any specific habitual behaviours that reflect what they used to say about you?

Do people in your life right now – friends and colleagues use any of the same phrases to describe you as your primary caregivers did? Have they been trained to view you in a specific way and have you been operating through the filter of these beliefs about yourself?

Are there any particular ways of thinking, speaking and behaving that you can adopt which can shift you out of any negative patterns that have been adopted based on your early conditioning?

Peer Pressure

What your peers thought about you during your prepubscence and adolescence can shape the image that you see in your internal mirror for the rest of your life, if you allow it to.

Sometimes we may diminish ourselves by playing down our talents, by being self-deprecating or hiding our light under a bushel to protect ourselves from the jealousy of others. In order to belong, we feel that we have to stop ourselves from standing out and hide any quirks or unique traits so that we can fit in with our peers.

Adolescence is the stage in our life cycle when the Crabs in the Bucket phenomenon, Tall Poppy Syndrome and Dog in the Manger mania takes hold with a vengeance. At this stage of our life, we are keen to fit in with our peers, follow the crowd, be accepted and belong. During our teenage years, we see our friends as part of our identity.

In many cultures, teenagers want to be separate and independent from their original family but they want to hang on to that feeling of belonging. That is why so many young people are drawn to gangs, searching for a sense of kinship outside of their immediate family circle. The collective worldview of your particular "gang" (or clique, sorority, fraternity, social group) may have become your worldview during that time.

Whether the opinions of your childhood and adolescent acquaintances were valid, kind, cruel or painful and whether or not you accepted or rejected their opinions, how you reacted to them has shaped a crucial part of your identity.

Are there any beliefs about your self-image and your abilities that have been handed to you by your friends from childhood and adolescence? Do any of these beliefs conflict with the goal that you wish to achieve? Do any of these beliefs need a desperate update?

Do you have any specific habitual **thoughts** about yourself which echo the attitudes of your friends and peers during childhood and adolescence (both positive and negative)?

Are there any **phrases** about yourself that you use which reflect the attitudes of your childhood peers (both positive and negative)?

Do you have any specific habitual **behaviours** that reflect what they used to say about you?

Do people in your life right now – friends and colleagues use any of the same phrases to describe you as your schoolmates or former childhood acquaintance did? Have you been operating through the lens of these past beliefs about yourself?

101

Are there any specific **new** ways of thinking, speaking and behaving that you can adopt which can shift you out of any negative patterns that have been adopted based on your early conditioning?

What you may have believed about yourself as a child or teenager, you don't need to believe about yourself as an independent adult.

The Pygmalion Effect

We accept the opinions of people who are in authority (such as doctors, scientists, teachers, parents) to be fact.

Even if we consciously or openly disagreed with our teachers when we were growing up, we may have <u>unconsciously</u> accepted and absorbed their opinions and expectations of us as if it were holy law.

In 1968, Robert Rosenthal (psychologist) and Lenore Jackson (elementary school principal) wrote a book based on their research called *Pygmalion in the Classroom.*

In their study, students took intelligence pre-tests. Then a random group of students were selected with no relation to their test results. The teachers were told that this random group of students showed unusual potential and academic promise. Eight months later, the random group of students was tested again and all of the students in the group performed at a significantly higher level.

The Pygmalion Effect is the term now given to the phenomenon where students perform in the way that teachers would expect them to perform even if the teachers are wrong about their students' capabilities. It refers to the way that students internalize and take on the positive and negative labels that are given to them by their teachers, regardless of whether the labels are accurate or not. The labels become a self-fulfilling prophecy. The higher the expectations, the better the student performs academically and the lower the expectations a teacher has, the worse the student performs.

What your teachers and other adults thought about you when you were growing up and how you were treated, whether it was valid or not, whether or not you accepted it or rejected it, may have shaped your identity.

Are there any ideas handed to you by your childhood teachers that could be blocking you from moving towards your goal?

Do you have any specific habitual **thoughts** about yourself which echo the attitudes of your teachers and bosses (both positive and negative)?

Are there any **phrases** about yourself that you use which reflect the attitudes of your teachers and bosses (both positive and negative)?

Do you have any specific habitual **behaviours** that reflect what they used to say about you or say about you now?

Do people in your life right now – friends and colleagues use any of the same phrases to describe you as authority figures have done? Have they been trained to view you in a specific way and have you been operating in life through the filter of these beliefs about yourself?

Are there any specific ways of thinking, speaking and behaving that you can adopt which can shift you out of any negative patterns that have been adopted based on your early conditioning?

There may be a temptation here to play the blame game and to feel angry or resentful about the way you may have been treated by your elders when you were young and vulnerable. But this would be disempowering. The aim of the questions above is to enable you to let go and release the erroneous or unhelpful opinions that people may have expressed to you rather than to be swallowed up by them again. They are invisible blocks that can hold you back. Busting through them can help you to move forward.

These exercises are not about trying to repair any perceived "damage" from the past. Their aim is to ensure that negative experiences and feelings from our past, don't determine and continue to influence our future.

In moving forward from the past, remember the wise words of Eleanore Roosevelt, *"No one can make you feel inferior without your consent!"*

Me and My Shadow

"This thing of darkness I acknowledge mine."
The Tempest
William Shakespeare

Sometimes people say, "I'm a positive thinker but negative things keep happening to me."

If you fall into this category, firstly, watch your words. The statement, "Negative things keep happening to me" acts like an instruction to your unconscious and you will continue to perceive that negative things keep happening to you.

Secondly, if you are thinking positive thoughts but negative things keep happening, you are probably ignoring or repressing your shadow self.

Our shadow self is a psychological term for our darker side. The shadow self is the home of the flaws, weaknesses, frailties, foibles, negative feelings and thoughts that we repress. It is made up of the parts of our personality that we find unacceptable or that we try to hide from others or our self.

However your Shadow Self is one of your greatest teachers, revealing to you your blocks and telling you where you need to grow and develop. It is your lifelong silent companion, just like your guardian angel. You can never get rid of your shadow. The Shadow Self is not to be eliminated but integrated. So honour your Shadow. Respect it. Don't shun it or it will keep showing up in the circumstances of your life at inconvenient moments to make its presence known.

Carl Jung said that "that which remains unconscious appears in our life as fate". He also said, "...what if I should discover that the...most impudent offenders are all within me...that I myself am the enemy...what then?"

And remember the other old saying, "If you ignore your shadow and from it try to hide, it will come back to haunt you and bite your poor backside."

Sometimes we only see our shadow self in our internal mirror instead of our whole self.

Some forms of therapy are based around integrating the shadow self with the rest of the self.

If you only see a flawed being in your internal mirror instead of an individual with an equal helping of both strengths and weaknesses, positive qualities and unhelpful habits, this will also serve to dent the level of your self-esteem.

Mirror Exercise

The following exercise is designed to integrate your aspirational self with the reflection that you "see" in your internal psychological mirror.

> You are standing in front of a large full-length mirror. Your reflection is smiling. Your reflection's eyes are happy. The image in the mirror is healthy and radiant. The image is waving and holding a symbol which represents the realisation of your goal. You may hear the self in your internal mirror telling you about the consequences or positive ramifications of the realised goal. The image may tell you about the next step you should take in your road to manifestation.
>
> Then your reflection beckons to you. You step towards the mirror and the glass dissolves. You and the reflection become one and you feel your reflection's emotions of triumph, jubilation and fulfilment, the satisfaction of a job well done.
>
> You carry these feelings with you as you open your eyes.

Self-Care

It is beyond the immediate scope of this book to discuss health matters. But part of maintaining a healthy level of self-esteem involves nurturing and looking after your physical health and well-being. When we are very busy, we may neglect or pay less attention to our physical health.

It is important to ensure that you are well-hydrated and are getting enough sleep. Sleep is one of the roads to inspiration as well as one of the best ways of helping to maintain the healthy functioning of your brain and heart.

Nutrition and exercise are also essential for your overall health and well-being.

You are not defined by your appearance. Your identity encompasses more than what your body looks like.

But the level of respect you give to your body in terms of nutrition, exercise and sleep can often offer an indication about the level of respect and attention that you have for yourself.

If your body gives out on you, it will hold you back or stop you altogether.

Your body is the only one you have. It is your home while you are living on this planet. It is resilient and self-healing. But it can only take so much neglect and abuse. So make it your number one priority. And treat it with love and care.

Eight

Reconstructing your Self-Image

Our surface personality is a mask or costume that is composed of our parents', teachers, peers and authority figures' opinions, perceptions, fears and beliefs.

The costume that we personally fashion is the result of social conditioning and we sometimes only see the costume and forget about the real person behind the mask.

The costume is not our identity but only our self-image.

Our Authentic Self lies beneath the mask. Discovering our Authentic Self is a bit like peeling back the layers of an onion.

Sometimes we are afraid and ashamed of our Authentic Naked Self and try to cover it up with acceptable social clothing just as Adam and Eve attempted to cover themselves with fig leaves in the Garden of Eden.

In Ancient Egyptian theology, human beings were said to have five attributes: the name, the shadow, the physical body (*akh*), the life-force or animating spirit (*ka*) and what they considered to be the personality or soul (*ba*).

When we integrate the personality that lies on the surface with our innate Authentic Self, the results are powerful and transformation can be said to take place on a cellular level.

In the book, *Simple Abundance,* author Sarah Ban Breathnach refers to DNA as our Destiny, Nature and Aspirations.

We have already discussed the idea that "who we *think* we are determines the course of our destiny."

Sometimes we equate or define ourselves according to the amount of possessions that we have. We judge ourselves according to whether we have the latest gadgets, the type of home we live in, the type of car we drive, the kind of clothes that we wear or by our parents' social class and economic status.

Other people define themselves by what they do for a living, their qualifications, their income or what they have or have not achieved in life.

Sometimes we can only see ourselves as others see us and so we define ourselves according to other people's opinions of ourselves, our social standing or our reputation.

Some people identify themselves exclusively with a leader or a cult, an idea, a religion or a particular set of beliefs. Consequently they have difficulty separating their identity from what or who they believe in and so if somebody challenges their beliefs – say for an example, an atheist challenges Christianity – one Christian may feel as if he is being personally criticised and feel defensive or angry. Whereas another Christian, whose personal identity is not so tied up with what he believes, would not feel threatened and would be able to engage and even enjoy debating with the atheist. His sense of self also would not depend on being able to convert or convince the atheist of the validity of his arguments.

Many people, especially females, but nowadays increasingly males, define themselves by the way that they look, by their society's standards of beauty or by the shape and size of their bodies.

Large numbers of people identify themselves with an emotional state of mind such as anger, depression, sadness or excitement. Other people define themselves, or allow others to define them, by their characteristics such as "boisterous", "shy", "outgoing" or "cantankerous".

In reality, we are not always one particular way. We display different characteristics depending on the relationship, context or circumstances of a given situation. Even though we are all multi-faceted beings, we tend to have one primary adjective or characteristic that we use to describe ourselves – most of the time, this is a label bestowed upon us by other people.

When you choose to align yourself with the labels that other people stick on you, it becomes like an unspoken covenant where you say, "Yes. I agree. That is me."

A child is like a blank canvas. They don't know who they are until a significant adult in their life tells them or sticks a label on them. "Oh, so that's who I am." Even if the adult is wrong in their opinion, the child will behave according to that label. It acts as an instruction and they are loyal to that description, perhaps for the rest of their life, even though they may have forgotten why they were given the original label in the first place.

If you are at a loss as to why you are having difficulty manifesting your goals, it could be that the labels that you have been given or that you have adopted as your own are at odds with what you want to create for yourself.

So once again, how do you mainly define yourself? Do you label yourself according to your income or your job description or your nationality or your ethnicity? Do you define yourself according to your age or what you look like? Do you view yourself mainly how other people see you?

What do you believe to be the primary source of your identity? If someone was to ask, "Who are you?" – aside from your name, what would be the first adjective or noun you would use to describe yourself?

When we define or label ourselves according to either our lack of possessions, our income, our job description (particularly if we hate our job), our educational background, a particular emotion, our reputation or our looks and size (even if we like what we see in the mirror), we are limiting ourselves. We are not seeing the full picture.

And if we are very successful in one of these areas and then suddenly lose that success through events or circumstances, we may feel as if we have lost our identity.

Detachment, in this context, means separating your identity from what you have, do, earn or look like. When you detach yourself from these factors, you are no longer limited. You are no longer in a box. There is no longer a glass ceiling or a social barrier. Solutions are instantly implementable and anything is possible. We become more than the thoughts we think, the emotions we feel and the bodies that we inhabit.

Nothing is static. What you have, do, earn or look like is only a temporary state and can change at any time. If you are consciously in the driving seat, you can help to change your circumstances for the better.

Once you have detached your identity from these factors, you can form a new identity based and organised around what you want to achieve.

Detachment from the Future

"If you can dream but not make your dreams your master..."

Rudyard Kipling

One of the paradoxes of manifestation is to remain detached from the outcome. This is a big challenge – especially if you are working hard towards something that you fervently desire. You don't want all that blood, sweat and tears to go to waste. It is hard to stay open to the possibility that things may not turn out exactly as you planned, in the timeframe that you were expecting or in the order that you intended. It is a difficult balancing act where you have to juggle between complete commitment to your cause and yet total detachment from the expected results. It involves playing your part but letting go of your attachment to the eventual outcome and having faith that Infinite Intelligence is supporting you and will take you to where you want to go – but not always in the way that you think things should happen.

If you have a strong attachment to things happening in a certain way, you may mistake temporary setbacks for failure and prematurely give up.

The judges on the TV programme *Masterchef* often say that, "The road to Masterchef glory is littered with the corpses of failed soufflés".

Rushing the manifestation process is a bit like opening an oven too early and ruining your cake.

Detachment from other people's opinions

This is generally the stage in your project where you will be asking for feedback and advice about your progress towards your goal.

We are very much influenced by crowd psychology. Emotions are particularly infectious. The influence of the collective community can magnify and intensify emotion, fortune and fate for good or for ill, for better or for worse.

Because humans are tribal creatures by nature, there tends to be a shared agreement within countries, cultures, neighbourhoods, colleagues, friends and families about the way things are - a shared view of reality.

When expanding our concept of reality, we may encounter many naysayers and it can be very challenging not to buy into the sometimes rigid perspectives of society.

Linguist and psychologist, S.I. Hayakawa said, "If you see in any given situation only what everybody else can see, you can be said to be so much a representative of your culture that you are a victim of it."

We can pretend that the Earth is flat just because everyone around us says it is, but at some stage in the manifestation process, we have to become independently minded. For some people, the fear of encountering disapproval within their community outweighs their desire to manifest their goals and dreams.

Other people's opinions are valid but they are to be taken as their opinions rather than facts and weighed up and assessed impartially. Take their opinions on board according to their particular perspective or expertise.

You can't achieve anything in isolation without some help from others. However you can't take other people's opinions as gospel. It is a balancing act where you have to put your own feelings and ego aside and hear others out but yet listen to them with an impartial ear, always remembering that they are talking from a particular viewpoint.

Don't seek advice from acquaintances that have a habit of dissing you or being overly critical or sceptical. Similarly, don't seek feedback and critique from acquaintances who are your biggest supporters and cheerleaders as they are not likely to be impartial either. Let them continue to be your biggest supporters and to enjoy what you are doing and to enjoy supporting you.

You also have to detach yourself from the notion of needing to prove other people wrong about you. Separate your need of wanting to prove people wrong from the actual goal itself. People may or may not change their opinion of you for the better if you accomplish your goal or ambition. But doing something solely out of a need to impress others can lead to disappointment and emptiness even if you succeed.

Detachment from your Past

"History," Stephen said, "is a nightmare from which I am trying to awake."'

Ulysses, James Joyce

We also can become very attached to our past. We create a story or a mythology or shape our history in a way that creates reasons and builds evidence as to why we can't achieve what we want to achieve.

Confabulation is the psychological process that occurs when gaps in the memory are filled with detailed, plausible but fictional explanations. Experts say that the process occurs unintentionally and unconsciously.

Even though we personally may not suffer from the memory or psychological disorders where confabulation occurs, to a lesser extent, we may use confabulation to rationalise our habits, our mindset, our way of doing things or our lack of achievements.

We are all gifted in the art of self-deception. There is sometimes a big difference between an event that happened and our story about what happened. We give it meaning and context and interpret the event according to our worldview and our self-image. This is why the same events can be described so differently by two people.

Part of the work involved in manifestation psychology involves facing up to the parts of our self that aren't so socially acceptable, evolved, nice and good. But in working with our shadow selves, we have to avoid beating ourselves up, punishing ourselves or feeling guilty. The work of manifestation psychology involves observing a negative pattern of thought, speech or behaviour that usually results in a negative outcome - and then changing the pattern of thought, behaviour or speech when it arises under similar circumstances the next time so that the outcome is better.

We also create dogmas out of our resentments. Negative emotions can be very addictive, accumulative and obsessive.

If we have a chronic illness or condition, we may define our core identity according to a medical diagnosis.

If we have suffered at the hands of others through abuse, bullying, violence or crime, we may define ourselves according to the way that we have been treated.

Labels can be a prison that box us in and restrict us. We work hard to protect our beliefs about ourselves, often enclosing these beliefs in a hard unbreakable outer casing. We cherish, nurture and sustain our negative labels.

We often become addicted to the dramas of our lives, like a character in one of the British soap operas that keeps making the same mistakes and never changes: different episode, same old script. I am reminded of the character Ian Beale in the TV programme *EastEnders*. Since 1985, this character has been chasing after, proposing to or marrying a succession of blonde beauties who always end up betraying him in one way or another. As I write, the character is now probably having his fiftieth nervous meltdown. But it is not an unrealistic characterisation. In reality, we often repeat the same patterns and storylines throughout our lives until we notice the behaviour that causes the pattern and in so doing, we break the spell.

If a negative story, memory, emotion, trauma or mindset becomes part of your identity, you start to feel as if it is who you are and then it becomes harder to let go of it because deep down you feel that by releasing the story, you would be losing the biggest part of yourself, your *modus operandi* and your *raison d'etre*. We are sometimes intensely loyal to our pain. It becomes, as Princess Diana once described the experience of having an eating disorder, a "shameful friend".

Energy flows in patterns and comes into being as Fate. Sometimes negative stories are inherited and passed down from generation to generation as a kind of fatalistic curse which threatens to haunt each descendant of the family with each successive generation suffering a similar fate at the same age. But you do not have to "live out your lineage", as they say.

The idea is not to forget the past, to disregard painful memories, to diminish other people's poor treatment of us or to ignore medical diagnoses. Rather it is recommended that we avoid moulding the bad things that have happened to us into our essential identity. We can view past challenges as something that we experienced rather than something that makes us who we are, as something that affected us deeply but that we are in the process of transcending. In this way, we can avoid being psychologically trapped by the past, by our history, by our health challenges or by the way that other people have treated us.

From Victim to Victor

Write a short autobiography (perhaps about a page or two long) describing the problems, situations and challenges that you have faced in your life - but from the point of view of how you overcame, conquered and transcended the difficulties that beset you. Also include a brief description of your accomplishments, achievements and strengths. This exercise can help to shift the mindset from victimhood to victory.

Don't Look Back in Anger

One of our biggest blocks which can stand in the way of us manifesting our dreams is an attitude of resentment, blame and negativity about the past. These emotions can really create a barrier, delay manifestation or even stop it from happening altogether. The good stuff belonging to the future can't get into your life because the mind and body is so consumed with all the bad stuff from the past.

When working through the previous chapter, some resentments or old wounds related to the words and attitudes of your primary caregivers, peers or authority figures during childhood and adolescence may have risen to the surface.

Although it wasn't our fault that these things may have happened to us, it is our responsibility to move on and not stay stuck in those experiences by allowing them to define our life.

Releasing our attachments to these wrongs doesn't necessarily mean pardoning or letting people off the hook for their poor behaviour. Releasing, in this context, means allowing the pain of the horrible things that have happened to you to leave your body.

From personal experience, I do know that after I have forgiven or let something go, something good always happens from another direction, usually in an unrelated area, but good fortune always results.

Sometimes forgiveness is more of an ongoing process than a finite event.

It is often taught that Nature abhors a void. On an energetic level, once you release past negative events, it leaves space for positive things to come into your life.

The Creative Use of Anger

Anger is not a negative or bad emotion in itself. It can be a force for good and an agent of change. For example, there is the

115

righteous anger that people experience when they witness social injustice or inequality.

On an individual psychological level, anger gives us information about the ways in which we don't want to be treated and where we need to set our boundaries. At its best, anger gives you guidelines about the experiences that you don't want to repeat. It is instructive. If we feel violated or betrayed or let down by others, we need to re-examine or retrace the steps that we ourselves took to get to that point so that we don't repeat the same mistakes again. This is the only point of analysis and of looking back at a painful "story" – to ensure that we don't experience the same situation again. What we don't remember, repeats itself.

The suppression of anger can cause depression. The expression of anger can cause mayhem and be destructive. But we don't want to eliminate anger. We want to manage it. People don't go on Anger Elimination courses. They go to Anger Management classes.

Anger is a powerful energy and can be a positive instrument of lasting transformation.

We can use our anger as fuel or as a catalyst for creativity. You can channel or redirect the energy of anger by transforming it either through writing it out in a journal, drawing it or expressing it as poetry or music if you are of a creative bent (or even if you aren't). Nobody need see these creative works that are an outlet for your rage, if you don't want them to.

If you prefer, you can write an angry letter about how you feel about the situation to the persons involved, saying exactly what you want to say or have fantasised about saying (but don't actually post or send the letter. I made this mistake once. Awkward!)

The person that you write to does not need to be in your life anymore. They don't even need to be alive anymore. After you have written the letter, ceremoniously rip or burn it up (or delete it if you have typed it). Erasing the letter is a symbol of the fact that you are no longer going to let that issue run riot in your mind.

The less energy that we spend focusing on past events, hurts and desires for revenge, the more energy we will have to keep us moving towards the manifestation of our goals.

Remember the words of Confucius: "Before you embark on a journey of revenge, dig two graves."

Lester Levenson

During the forties and early fifties, Lester Levenson was a successful businessman who suffered a series of chronic and debilitating health challenges including ulcers which perforated his stomach, an enlarged liver, problems with his spleen, kidney stones and heart trouble.

Finally in 1952, when he was only 42, he suffered a second heart attack and was told that he had about two weeks left to live, if he was lucky.

He was sent home to get his affairs in order and told to avoid any physical exertion as this would shorten the already little time he had left.

Lester Levenson engaged in a period of reflection, a daily practice of letting go and releasing himself from all of his negative emotions, ideas and memories. By the end of three months, he was completely healed of all his diseases. Instead of dying in two weeks, he lived for another forty-two years.

Lester Levenson's story illustrates, not only, the power of releasing, but how emotions can live in the body and alter its condition for better or for worse.

Forgiveness versus Release

The word "Forgiveness" sometimes has associations or connotations with pardoning people for what they have done, letting them off the hook or condoning bad behaviour.

But if we think of forgiveness in terms of releasing negative energy from our body rather than excusing other people's mistreatment, abuse, abandonment or cruelty, it can help us to transcend the idea that by forgiving someone, we are letting them "get away with it".

117

This process removes the other person from the equation and allows us to focus on the impact that a particular incident has had on our emotions, our energy, our mind and our body. It then allows us to release the incident from our energy field, from our psyche and from our body.

Part of letting go also means letting go of the desire for the perpetrator to understand how much pain they have caused or letting go of the need to get an apology. When we "forgive the debtor" or let the experience go, the compensation that we will receive from the Universe will exceed the original debt.

Letting go of past wrongs and hurts doesn't mean that you have to let toxic people back into your life or get close to them again. It means dissolving the negative charge that may occur whenever you think about them or the events that affected you adversely so that whenever it crosses your mind, you feel neutral and almost indifferent.

Guilt can also be a powerful block to manifestation. If you are secretly punishing or berating yourself for things you have done or shouldn't have done, deep down you will believe that you do not deserve to be successful.

Sometimes to speed up the manifestation process, the most important person that you have to forgive is yourself.

The Power of Guided Imagery

Guided imagery is based on the theory that the mind and the body are deeply connected.

The reason it works as a relaxation tool or healing method is because the Home of the Shadow Self cannot differentiate between the images that originate from actual memories and the images that are only invented or that aren't actually taking place in the physical world.

This is why imagined or irrational fears, worries or the fear of things that haven't happened yet, can create the same physiological reactions in the body as frightening experiences and traumas that are actually occurring.

118

For example, someone who is convinced that their house is haunted, even though they haven't seen any ghosts, might experience reactions symptomatic of panic such as sweating, trembling, palpitations or shallow breathing.

Someone with a lifelong fear of public speaking who has to deliver a presentation to twenty people may also experience the same physiological reactions whilst delivering their speech.

And someone who is actually being chased by a wild animal through a dark forest in the middle of the night might also experience the same physiological reactions.

Only one of the people in these three scenarios is in actual physical danger but the strength of the emotions of all three people means that their body is experiencing similar physical side effects.

When the flight-or-fight response is initiated by the physiological processes of the body, we can't think clearly, our thoughts speed up and become overwhelming and our breathing becomes more rapid and shallow. Blood flows to the back of the brain where past memories are stored. Present challenges and problems will become linked with the past situations where things have gone wrong.

The power of the mind-body connection is the reason why we may begin to salivate when looking at a recipe book or smelling food – even though we're not eating. It's also the reason why a certain smell can make you mentally re-experience a painful or happy memory from your childhood.

Employing the use of guided imagery can help you to release emotions such as anger, frustration, rage, anxiety, overwhelm and fear.

Studies and experiments have shown that using guided imagery as a releasing tool can also help to:

- Reduce your stress significantly
- Relax your physical body
- Create a positive shift in your brainwave activity and your biochemistry
- Lower your blood pressure

- Reduce your cholesterol levels
- Reduce the levels of glucose in your blood
- Increase short-term immune cell activity
- And help you to get in touch with the "wiser part of yourself" (the Superconscious or the "Inner Genie")

Many people make the mistake of thinking that guided imagery only involves visual images.

But in fact, as discussed in Chapter Three, guided imagery can involve the use of ALL senses – including hearing, feeling, touch, smell and taste.

This is good news for people who may find it challenging to picture things with their mind. Because they may find it easier to imagine hearing sounds, or remembering feelings, smells or flavours.

If you think right now of the way that you re-experience your memories, you may get a clue as to which of your senses will be particularly strong when you practise guided imagery exercises.

For example, when you relive a memory, do you experience it in pictures or like a movie, or do you hear what was said or experienced? Do you remember the way something smells? Do songs that you hear on the radio cause you to travel back to a particular time in your life? Does a smell evoke a memory of your childhood? Or do you re-experience the emotions?

Maybe you experience a combination of sights, sounds and sensations when you relive a memory.

Which one is it for you?

In modern times, the fight response triggers the emotion of anger and flight response triggers the emotion of fear.

Where do you experience anger and fear in your body?

Do you have a constant background feeling of anger or fear as you go about your daily life?

Past experiences of abandonment, rejection, lack of control, hopelessness and helplessness tend to create emotions in present day situations which block the potential for manifesting goals as well as inducing stress.

Stress interrupts the functioning of the immune system making you vulnerable to illness, frustration and self-fulfilling disappointment.

Emotional Stress Release Technique

Emotional Stress Release techniques, sometimes known as ESR, have been developed in the field of kinesiology. Kinesiology is the study of body movement. It is particularly concerned with the muscles and nerves and how they affect the physiological processes, mental attitudes, emotional reactions, learning and behaviour. It's a holistic therapy which focuses on creating physical, emotional, psychological and nutritional health, balance and well-being.

You can use the following adaptation of an emotional stress relief technique to detach yourself from any label, memory, story, anger or attitude that you believe is holding you back.

Think of a painful memory, emotion or attitude or restricting label that you feel is holding you back from achieving your goal.

(It's important that you only pick one challenge to work with at a time for the technique to have the most beneficial effect. If it's a big complex problem, just choose one aspect of the issue that is frustrating or upsetting you.)

When you think of this emotion, which part of your body is affected? Can you feel the emotion actually sitting in that part of your body? Or maybe you feel it outside of your body but nestling around you inside of your personal energetic field or aura?

If this memory, emotion, attitude or label was a colour, what would it be?

If this memory, emotion, attitude or label was a sound, what would you hear?

If it was a taste or smell, what would you experience?

If it was a shape, what would it look like?

If it was a texture, what would it feel like?

See this image sitting in the area of your body or the part of your personal energetic field that is affected by that emotion. If it has a sound or smell, experience that sound or smell in your imagination.

Then watch this image being surrounded by a big clear bubble. The bubble gently lifts the image out of your body or energy field and floats far away. The bubble and the image within it gradually begins to shrink until it POPS and dissolves into nothing.

Repeat this exercise whenever you need to and notice the changes you feel not only in your emotions but in your body.

We carry the pain of the wrongs that have been committed against us inside the cellular memory of our body's organs. It can lead to emotional constipation which in turn leads to severe physical illnesses or conditions such as depression.

The body is the home of our unconscious and our shadow self. Part of our mind is located in the energy storage centres of our body and not just in our brain. So even if we don't consciously remember negative things or don't think about them that much, our bodies remember. Our bodies house our hurts, shelter our grievances and nurse our betrayals. Our bodies carry our emotional pain. What we embody, we project into our future. Releasing negative energy from our body allows us to embody positivity and project that into the future instead.

The Wisdom of Rest and Relaxation

Perhaps it is time to revisit the Rudyard Kipling poem from the opening chapter of this book:

I keep six honest serving-men:
(They taught me all I knew)
Their names are What and Where and When
And How and Why and Who.
I send them over land and sea,
I send them east and west;
But after they have worked for me,
I give them all a rest.

We already discussed this in Chapter Four but it is worth repeating here because in the age of Information Overload, it is so counter-intuitive: The three 'R's: Rest, Relaxation and Renewal make us more productive, not less.

This is a modern challenge as many of us are reluctant to rest. Sleep is seen as an unproductive waste of time. We feel as if we have so much to do and so little time to do it in. "There aren't enough hours in the day...if only I could clone myself," we often say. We keep running on empty until we burn out.

In order to juggle your many roles such as employee, entrepreneur, parent, volunteer, spouse etc. without feeling guilty and overstretched, one day a week of doing nothing but relaxing is crucial to keep you motivated for the rest of the week.

When you *are* working or engaged in creative activity, take a break every ninety minutes.

The body performs self-healing actions such as repairing and replacing cells or strengthening the immune system during relaxation, meditation, rest and sleep as well as balancing out stressful emotions. Spending time in nature also helps to balance and reset our emotions.

Our minds are also more open to further unconscious inspiration and ideas during relaxation, meditation, rest and sleep. We may also receive or unconsciously work out solutions to challenges during this period of downtime.

Relaxation, rest, meditation and sleep also help to create, strengthen and sustain mental and emotional clarity.

The three Rs help us to reduce the risk of depression, stress and daily lethargy. We clear out our mental, emotional and physical toxins during this period of downtime.

The body also resets, rebalances and renews itself during movement and exercise.

Honour and obey the processes and deeper needs of your body and in the long run, you will be more productive.

The three Rs help us to enjoy our work and enjoy the journey.

Releasing the Old

Just as forgiveness creates a spiritual vacuum for you to receive abundance and good fortune, so too does creating a physical vacuum.

When you get rid of the clutter that you have been hoarding, give away things that you no longer need, throw out rubbish or donate clothes and books to worthwhile causes, you are creating the physical space to receive more good in your life on all levels including the emotional, the material, the spiritual and the mental.

Also the less cluttered your environment is, the less cluttered your mind will be and the more motivated and inspired you will become.

Releasing the old can also mean letting go of people who create a negative drain on your energy and gently transitioning them out of your life.

There must be an ongoing removal of the worn-out and outdated in your life for you to attract the new resources, prosperous relationships, novel ideas and exciting new contacts that will transform your dreams into a new reality.

Gate Three

Manifesting Magic

Gate 3

Introduction

The word 'psychology' first meant the study of the psyche.

Psyche, from the Greek, is usually translated as *mind* or *soul*. It literally means "animating spirit" or the life force that occupies the physical body.

The character Psyche, in Greek mythology, is usually depicted with butterfly wings.

The butterfly is a symbol of the soul and it also contains the idea of transformation (i.e. the journey from caterpillar to butterfly).

To manifest can mean to reveal or display. Manifestation can also mean "visible expression".

Manifestation Psychology can therefore be described as the revelation, unfolding or visible expression of the soul.

At the transpersonal or universal level, the psychology of manifestation is a study of human potential, of what is possible and achievable, not only for the benefit of the individual, but also for that of humankind.

In *Manifesting Magic*, we explore ways to activate the untapped powers of our mind, ways to co-create our future with the powerful Energetic Life Field that surrounds us and ways to connect with the collective wisdom of humanity in order to achieve our goals.

Nine

The Powers of Your Mind

"I began to think of the soul as if it were a castle made of a single diamond or of very clear crystal, in which there are many rooms, just as in Heaven, there are many mansions."

Interior Castle, Teresa of Avila

Self Concept v. 2.0

We are all multidimensional beings. Depending on our culture or how we have been brought up, we tend to project most of our positive qualities, attributes, powers and gifts on to the image of either:

(i) A divine (usually patriarchal), omniscient creator or

(ii) A political (usually patriarchal) figure, or government body or

(iii) A celebrity (usually female e.g. the Nation's sweetheart, the People's Princess)

We have been given the power to create our destiny and be the architect of our own lives although our individual circumstances and starting points may vary vastly. Indeed some members of the human "race" could be described as having a huge headstart over others.

Nevertheless we have been endowed with the gift of free will. But for the most part, we do not consciously use our power. Instead we often project our own power onto our designated leaders and the iconic figures in our cultures. We then become confused and annoyed when these people stumble under the weight of our vicarious expectations and topple off their pedestal.

We need to accept and embrace the power lying dormant within us as it is our right to use.

We can also choose to learn (or remember) how to work and collaborate with this Spiritual and Universal Source in order to co-create and manifest what we have envisioned.

"In my Father's house, there are many mansions...."

There are six core dimensions of the mind. Knowing how to *intentionally* access these different dimensions of the mind for specific aims can lead to greater accomplishment, achievement, success and fulfilment.

The six main dimensions of the mind are:

(i) The Home of the Shadow Self (or the Basement)
(ii) The Storehouse of Knowledge
(iii) The Dimension of the Present Moment (Conscious awareness)
(iv) The Psyche of the Human Community (or the collective unconscious)
(v) The Inner Genie (or the Gateway to Spirit)
(vi) Infinite Intelligence (or the Divine)

The Home of the Shadow Self

This is the home of our buried memories, concealed fears and unconscious habits.

These habits were formed as a reaction to the way that we were treated by parental figures, peers and authority figures in our formative years.

These habits include repetitive ways of thinking as well as our characteristic patterns of behaviour. It is the part of ourselves that we tend to exile or disconnect.

Guilt resides in the Home of the Shadow Self and so does our Conscience. When we experience a Dark Night of the Soul, we are resonating with the Home of the Shadow Self.

The Shadow Self is not very good at discriminating. It has a very simplistic, childlike, black-and-white perspective. Some of its ideas were formed during infancy at the pre-verbal stage of development so it sometimes has difficulty articulating feelings and emotions.

The Shadow Self is governed by our "reptilian" brain so it responds instinctively to situations and panics when its needs cannot be immediately satisfied. The Shadow Self is governed by the past but feels all these emotions in the present. It thinks rigidly and behaves compulsively.

The Shadow Self is the oldest part of you (in that it has been with you since childhood) but it is also the youngest part of you, because it hasn't evolved from childhood. It can be viewed as the dark side of your Inner Child.

Just as children can be cruel and blunt, the voice of the Shadow Self tends to hit uncomfortable nerves and bruise the overall ego. The Shadow Self is your internal critic and likes to give you a bad review. It challenges, accuses, berates, insults and abuses, often in a disguised internal voice that sounds like a parent or some other authoritative adult. But in actual fact, this is the voice of a wounded child that is only echoing what he or she believes they have heard about themselves, others and life.

The Shadow Self cannot discern the difference between what is true and what is not, what is imagined and what is real. It is vulnerable to paranoia. It takes all information at face value. It believes everything it hears. It doesn't understand the subtleties of humour and irony. It can also be very reactive.

But because it cannot distinguish between the real and the imagined, it is an excellent aid to manifestation because its beliefs are so strong. When you nourish the Shadow Self with images of success and visions of your intended goal, it takes these images literally and interprets them as fact.

Repeating affirmations sometimes doesn't work as well with the Shadow Self as visualisation does. It interprets images as real. But it will challenge and contradict positive verbal statements. Visualisation and emotions tend to bypass this part of the mind that likes to contradict and challenge the positive statements that you might try to feed the psyche.

The Home of the Shadow Self is a very valuable part of the mind because it provides us with the information that allows us to heal our wounds. However the Shadow Self cannot be left to run our psyche. A two year old is a beloved and treasured member of his or her family. But if the whims and the tantrums of the two year old are allowed to govern the family, the effects would be chaotic, and even destructive, for all concerned. The Shadow Self is like a two year old child that must not be ignored, neglected or mistreated but yet must not be in charge.

Information often has to be sifted through the conscious and superconscious parts of the mind in order to be interpreted with more accuracy. However the Home of the Shadow Self is the road to healing at all levels. The Home of the Shadow Self can then be safely transformed into the Home of the Inner Child. Because the child you once were never leaves you. You carry him or her with you wherever you go.

The Storehouse of Knowledge

The Storehouse of Knowledge records everything that we have ever seen, felt, experienced and learnt. It is like a huge archive, library or supercomputer.

This Knowledge Base also includes our innate skills, talents and gifts as well as those that we acquire through education, training and working.

Skills that we perform unconsciously such as driving a car are also stored here.

This information remains in an unconscious state in our archives. But it is not buried or hidden. It can be retrieved as and when we need it.

The Storehouse of Knowledge focuses more on interpreting non-verbal communication and interaction (such as body language, gestures and facial expressions).

It is the part of the mind that is most fluent at understanding the subtleties of body language and visual cues. It picks up telepathic information about other people that we are barely aware of consciously because it digests information so quickly.

When we meet someone for the first time, we assess whether or not we like or trust them. The Storehouse of Knowledge makes this decision based on the information in the archives (in other words, life experience to date).

The Storehouse of Knowledge is the realm of those sophisticated and complex mirror neurons, the brain cells that specialise in understanding and imitating the behaviours of those around us.

This part of the mind makes decisions and then transmits this information to the conscious mind. It makes snap decisions in a matter of seconds based on our worldview, self-image and life experience. It is not an infallible part of the mind because its source of Knowledge is mostly based on past experience.

The Storehouse of Knowledge is governed by our "limbic" brain. Our limbic brain records the memories of pleasurable and painful experiences which in turn influences our emotions and our value judgements.

133

The Storehouse of Knowledge also holds copies of its data in the cells of our bodies. Thus our cells, tissues and organs store memories of our experiences. This information can be a source of wisdom. However it is not infallible. Some of the information contains errors of judgement, errors in perception and skewed perceptions of past experiences.

Philosopher and psychologist William James described the mind as an "associating machine". He stated that our whole thought process hinges on association and that new images, sensations, thoughts or interpretations of events are always associated with information that already exists in the mind, information based on past experiences.

This means that if left unchecked, our past experiences will influence how we interpret current events. If, for example say, the colour orange was involved in a painful memory, the colour orange may continue to create stress during current events that have no other connection with the original painful memory.

A powerful example of the effect of memory is illustrated in the TV biopic *Seeing Red,* based on the book of the same name, where actress turned foster mother Coral Atkins describes how a childhood trauma linked with the colour red had rendered her physically unable to see the colour red from then on.

Our interpretation of current events in our daily life and in our society shapes our opinions and our world view. Our interpretations, if based on past evidence and not on what is actually going on before us, can create a barrier to opportunity.

In short, our memory and our interpretation of things past determine how we see the world – it shapes and moulds our reality.

The Dimension of the Present Moment

This is basically the dimension of the five physical senses. So it encompasses everything that we can see, hear, touch, smell and taste right now. It includes all the sensations that we are experiencing in our physical body as we experience them. It also includes all the thoughts that we are thinking in the present moment.

As this dimension of the mind is focused in Time, it is very linear and we can only concentrate upon one thought or experience at a time.

Everything that we don't need in the Present Moment is either filed away in the Storehouse of Knowledge or buried in the Home of the Shadow Self.

The Psyche of the Human Community

This is the part of our mind that is connected to the minds of the other people in our local community, culture, nation, ethnicity and ancestry. It is the psyche of the human community, often described as the collective unconscious.

It is the home of ideas, inventions, philosophies, prejudices, collective fears and phobias, religious attitudes, stereotypical mindsets, archetypal images, iconography and symbols. This is the part of the mind that is influenced by advertising, propaganda and subliminal imagery.

This is the Storehouse of knowledge and Home of the Shadow Self combined for the whole human race. The home of both the Fairy Godmother and the Big Bad Wolf.

It holds our highest aspirations and virtues as well as our worst crimes against humanity and deepest collective flaws.

We tend to tune into the psyche of the human community when an event of huge enormity takes place such as the events of September 11, 2001. During such momentous or traumatic events, the collective fears and the imagination of the human population become heightened. We also tune into the Community of the Psyche when a great religious leader, larger than life political figure or iconic celebrity dies suddenly and unexpectedly making us all become aware of our own individual mortality.

Some of us are more connected to the Community's Psyche than others. Inventors, writers, psychics, therapists, psychologists, philosophers and artists resonate particularly well with the Psyche of the Human Community.

135

The Inner Genie

Transpersonal psychologists and therapists may call this part of the mind the "Superconscious" or the Archetypal Self.

I call it the "Inner Genie" and the "Gateway to Spirit" because I believe that it is the part of our mind that is closely connected to Divine Intelligence, the Cosmic Consciousness or what people understand as being "God."

Dr Jean Houston refers to this part of the mind as the Essential Self or *entelechy* (which can be described as our best, most wise and most compassionate self, that is already aware of our life path and soul purpose.)

Houston uses the example of it being the *entelechy* of an acorn to be an oak tree, or the entelechy of a seed to be a flower.

When we connect with our Essential Self, life's events and circumstances develop for us at a more organic level for our highest good.

The philosopher Aristotle invented the term *entelechy* to describe a sense of ongoing completion through activity, the fruition or manifestation of potential. In other words, you are the potential and your Essential Self is that potential fully realised and manifested. This *entelechy* is the essence of yourself at your highest, most evolved level of development.

When you contact and communicate with the Essential Self, your highest possibilities begin to emerge. The Essential Self is a wise, compassionate, understanding and empowering friend that can help you be all that you are capable of being, showing you how all the experiences you have had to date have brought you to where you are and how you can realise your highest level of possibility and purpose.

Other teachers call this part of the mind the "Evolutionary Self" because it is the most evolved part of our self. It is the part of the self that has never been wounded, betrayed, victimised or abandoned. It has never made mistakes. It is the part of the self that does not seek to impress others. It is the truth seeking part of us that gives us the impulse and the drive to be all that we can be and more.

This part of the self is sometimes called the Witness or the Observer.

The Gateway to Spirit is our hotline to a Higher Power, our pathway to enlightenment and connection with Divinity.

It is sometimes described as the "still small voice within". It is the voice of inspiration and intuition.

The Inner Genie is great at solving problems and creating solutions.

This part of the mind might communicate with us by drawing our attention to the pertinent lyrics of a song playing on the radio or to the book that falls off the shelf on a significant page or an overheard snatch of conversation that brings us an insight, gives us an idea or that helps us to arrive at a solution.

The flashes, hunches and gut feelings that we get are often communicated to us through our Inner Genie.

When the practice of repeating or writing positive affirmations works successfully, it is because the affirmations have resonated with the superconscious part of the mind.

All parts of the mind communicate to us when we sleep using the language of dreams. (Indeed the Home of the Shadow Self may give us nightmares). But the Inner Genie gives us dreams that create solutions.

The Inner Genie remains at work even if we are not consciously thinking about our goal, especially if we have written down a clear statement of intent.

Superconscious creativity occurs most frequently during the first hour upon awakening or when our brainwaves vibrate at a slower frequency when we are deeply relaxed. This brainwave frequency is known as the alpha state of consciousness.

Infinite Intelligence

This is the most powerful part of the mind where all possibilities lie dormant waiting to be manifested.

Infinite intelligence can blast a complete and brilliant idea into our conscious mind like a blinding flash - without being filtered through the usual route of the superconscious highway.

Communication from this part of the mind feels like a revelation or illumination. You feel energised and excited and ready for action. It can be like a headrush where you receive a lot of information all of a sudden.

This is the part of the mind that provides the "Eureka!" moments.

When we receive insights that are way beyond our life experience or educational background, we are receiving this information from the domain of Infinite Intelligence.

It is the dimension of the psyche that deals with Truth.

This is the part of the mind that creates coincidental and synchronistic experiences. It knows all the paths, can move all the pieces of the jigsaw, rearrange your circumstances and put the necessary people into your path for you to reach your ultimate destination.

Coincidences are teachers which can serve as signposts or guides. They are to be regarded as more than random chance, an amusing anecdote or an interesting curiosity. They should be seen as a communication from Infinite Intelligence. They are a message or a clue about areas of our lives or goals that need attention. We can stimulate and increase the frequency of coincidences by paying attention to every coincidence that occurs and using it as guide or clue about our next step.

Deepak Chopra writes in his book *Synchrodestiny* that the more that we pay attention to coincidences, the more they will occur.

"To coincide" means "to fit together". In geometry, "to coincide" means to arrive at the same point, to correspond exactly or to occupy the same place. Each coincidence contains a meaning and is a stepping stone. Even the smallest of coincidences may contain a hugely significant message.

Psychologist Carl Jung referred to coincidence as the "archetype of magical effect". He studied the phenomenon of "meaningful coincidences" and it is he who coined the term "synchronicity."

The American TV series *Touch* illustrates how events and disparate people are connected and their lives entwined through synchronistic events. So do concepts in popular culture such as "Six Degrees of Separation" (or indeed the "Six Degrees of Kevin Bacon".)

In the world of the Internet, a relatively new movement called Synchromysticism is flourishing. "Synchromystics" explore the hidden connections and strange coincidences that exist between popular culture (movies, music etc.), esoteric knowledge and current or historical events. This kind of exploration lies more in the domain of the psyche of the human community (a.k.a. the collective unconscious mind).

Infinite Intelligence is the orchestrator of Synchronicity. Synchronicity is usually described as the way that apparently unrelated events can form a pattern or connection which leads to a fortuitous outcome or result or solution. The connection between these events is not always immediately apparent. There is a Universal Order of Events but sometimes we are too close to these events to see the connections and so they may often seem bizarre and random.

Infinite Intelligence is the author of Serendipity. Serendipity is the word used to describe happy coincidences, which include, as mentioned earlier, insights found in casual telephone conversations, books that fall off the shelf, overheard conversation from strangers or the lyrics of a song on the radio that speak to your situation.

Unfortunately in the same way that we often disown our Shadow Self, we also disconnect ourselves from the part of our mind that is home to Divine Intelligence.

We often cast the Shadow Self in the role of the devil (as in "the Devil made me do it"), whereas Infinite Intelligence (or omniscience) may be interpreted by many as another way of describing "God". Stating that a part of our mind is connected to the Divine, may to some people, sound like grandiosity, delusion or even blasphemy.

139

We disconnect our minds from both ends of the spectrum – from the part of ourselves that we view as Evil and the part of ourselves that we see as Good or God.

Writer Gregg Braden believes that within each cell in every living being on the planet is encoded a genetic message. In his book, *The God Code,* he arrived at this message by linking the building blocks of our DNA (hydrogen, oxygen, nitrogen and carbon) with their numerical equivalents of the elements on the Periodic Table using gematria. He also linked these numbers with the corresponding letters of the Hebrew alphabet. The message he believes that is encoded in our cells (when translated from both the languages of DNA and Hebrew) is: *God/Eternal within the body.*

"Let us create man *in our image,*" God is translated as saying in the Book of Genesis. (According to some experts, the original Hebrew text actually reads, "And the Gods said, "*Let us remake man, after our image, and after our likeness...*")

In the New Testament (John 10:34), Jesus is attributed as saying, "Is it not written in your own scriptures that *you are gods?*"

And in 1 Corinthians 3:16, it reads, "Do you not realise that you are a temple of God with the Spirit of God living in you?"

There is also the Jewish Book of Haggadah which describes human beings as uniting both "heavenly and earthly qualities" within themselves.

Whatever label we choose to give it, Infinite Intelligence continues to operate in spite of ourselves. But sometimes Infinite Intelligence can't do "its thing" at the maximum level if we are not giving it our full attention or if we are getting in the way with too much unproductive activity. We need to pay full attention and listen to this Special Guest and then we will receive the answers that we need.

Infinite Intelligence responds to the focus of our consciousness, expectations and emotions. It performs like a kind of cosmic mirror that recreates a kind of metaphorical representation of our innermost thoughts, emotions and beliefs

140

in the outer world. Therefore infinite Intelligence is an interactive phenomenon.

These are the Six Core Dimensions of the Mind.

To activate healing and remove inner blocks to success or clean psychological wounds, we engage with the Home of the Shadow Self.

To inspire or be inspired, to lead by example, to empathise and to contribute to the world around us, we connect with the Psyche of the Human Community.

To activate our dormant genius gifts, receive guidance and intuitive knowledge about our next steps in life, we connect with our Inner Genie.

Infinite Intelligence will usually get in touch with us (rather than the other way around) so in this case, it is a matter of remaining alert and watching and listening for signals.

In the following chapter, we will explore ways that we can connect with our Inner Genie, the superconscious part of our mind that connects with Infinite Intelligence.

Ten

Activating your Inner Genius

When you access the inner dimensions of your mind and use the particular gifts that each dimension has to offer, you can:

- develop your intuition
- increase your creativity
- find solutions to problems
- make better decisions
- improve your memory
- accelerate physiological healing

By engaging both the left and right hemispheres of your brain, you can combine your intuitive skills with the rational faculty of the mind for effective and longer-lasting results.

One of the best ways to access these inner dimensions of the mind is to use self-hypnosis techniques. This is not as sinister as it may sound because we are all actually automatically hypnotising ourselves all the time with our most dominant thoughts.

Self-hypnosis is but one doorway to the inner conscious levels of the mind.

The Scottish surgeon, James Braid, who was an eye and muscle specialist, is considered to be the "father" of hypnosis. (Although there were many people who worked with subjects in the hypnotic state prior to Braid, including Franz Mesmer from where we get the words 'mesmerised' and 'mesmerism').

However it was James Braid who actually coined the term 'hypnosis', naming the process after Hypnos who was the Greek god of sleep. Braid initially thought that the hypnotic state was a form of sleep.

He later realised that his subjects were fully awake when hypnotised but just focused in another state of consciousness. He then tried to change the name but the term 'hypnosis' had already been embraced by mainstream culture.

But the point I want to emphasise is that hypnosis is not a form of sleep (although it can be used to induce sleep). Hypnosis is a change in the focus of your consciousness from the Dimension of the Present Moment to one of the inner levels of the mind. With this change of focus, you can access all the wisdom, intuition and gifts that the deeper mind contains.

Accessing these deeper levels can help artists, composers, writers, poets and painters to bust through their creative blocks and increase their confidence.

Activating your inner genius or inner genies in this way through an expansion of consciousness and imagination can, not only help you to manifest a successful future, but also aid you in the creation of your art, your business or your problem-solving abilities.

Some musicians, writers and artists often claim that they channel their creativity from another source. Sometimes they describe that source as "God". Some may use the term, "Angels". Others use the term "Higher Power" or "Higher Self".

The composer Mozart is one such example as is the writer Ralph Waldo Emerson. Beethoven claimed that he "transcribed" many of his great symphonies after he went deaf.

Michael Faraday, a mostly "self-educated" man, claimed to have received his information about scientific principles in a dream. His innovations led to the birth of the electronic industry and he is often described as one of the most influential scientists in history.

We all have the gift of genius lying dormant within us. It is just that relatively few of us know how to activate this power and most of the people that are in touch with their Inner Genius are not doing it intentionally but have stumbled upon it unconsciously, mostly through having a passionate interest in a particular discipline or through being deeply connected to a "past" life memory.

Your Subjective Inner Senses

All humans have subjective inner senses which correspond to our five physical senses.

Intuition means to "see within" or to have insight. However it literally means *in-tuition*, as in an Inner Tutor.

Our Inner Genie is always communicating with us, channelling information from Divine Intelligence. But our minds are often too cluttered to be able to listen to this inner wisdom.

Clairvoyance is often used as an umbrella term for all kinds of psychic experiences and abilities and the word 'clairvoyance' may conjure up images of creepy séances, Ouija boards, hysteria and fake mediums.

However within the context of manifestation psychology, the meaning is slightly different:

Clairvoyance means clear vision: intuition that involves the visual sense. This is a particularly strong inner sense for people who have an acute sense of colour and image, and who find it easy to see things with their mind's eye or to picture things from memory. They tend to have a strong sense of clarity.

Clairsentience means clear feeling: intuition that involves the kinaesthetic senses of feeling and physical sensations. People who have a strong kinaesthetic sense are sensitive to emotional atmospheres and emotional energy. They are very empathetic. They have a strong gut instinct. They receive intuitive communications primarily through their emotions, physiological reactions in their body and through their sense of touch. They may be drawn to forms of therapy involving Touch or Bodywork. They may be either very tactile and demonstrative or, at the other end of the spectrum, avoid physical contact

145

altogether because of their extreme sensitivity to touch. Touch is often believed to be a more powerful method of contact than verbal communication.

Clairaudience means clear hearing: intuition that involves the hearing sense. Auditory people have an acute outer sense of hearing. They receive intuitive communications via their own inner voice. They may be able to channel information, music, new ideas, poetry or stories via their superconscious.

The sense of smell is connected to emotional memory and the consciousness of the physical body where cellular information is stored.

It is a good idea to develop all your subjective inner senses to enhance your creative, entrepreneurial and communication skills as well as your level of empathy with others.

Our subjective inner senses are generally more underdeveloped than our physical senses. We don't tend to value or appreciate our subjective inner senses. We even talk about the imagination in a disparaging way at times.

But everything that exists in reality first existed in the imagination. As mentioned earlier in this book, Einstein once famously said that imagination was more important than knowledge.

One of the best ways of developing and strengthening our inner subjective senses is by enhancing and cultivating our physical senses of sight, sound, touch, smell and taste. In our information-saturated world, we tend to live in a virtual reality and are a little out of touch with our physical reality and senses. The senses of sight, sound, touch, smell and taste are not used to their full capacity.

Some people may focus too much on their inner world at the expense of their experiences in daily physical reality and thus feel isolated, adrift or as if they are not accomplishing or getting anything done.

Other people may concentrate too much on their external world, social events, the possessions they want and pay scant attention to their inner life. This may result in them feeling as if life is shallow, empty or as if something is missing.

Both ways of being are unbalanced. A well-developed inner world can enhance and improve your daily experience, social interaction and productivity in the outer world. A well-balanced connection with your environment, with other people, with work, hobbies and social activities can enrich and enhance your inner world.

Appreciating and consciously experiencing our physical senses in daily life (the Dimension of the Present Moment) and intentionally and purposefully using our senses to as full a capacity as we are able, will lead to an enlargement of both inner and outer consciousness. Revitalising the senses can even lead to an expansion of our intellectual skills as well as a new zest for life.

Social conditioning tells us that everything (including our health, intellect, well-being) goes downhill after the age of twenty-five. We are constantly told that our best years are behind us. This is a myth. Your senses can be as acute and as open and as vital as they were when you were five years old.

Opening yourself up to new cultural experiences, different taste sensations, or unusual (for you) styles of cuisine can help to revitalise your mind and in so doing enhance your creativity.

When you experience life through the eyes of a child or perhaps through the eyes of your own young son or daughter, you are expanding your creative imagination, your sensory memory, your ability to visualise and your capacity to generate ideas and insights.

Alter your daily routine, for example, by travelling via different routes. Pay attention to your environment. Look at the things, people, and places that you see every day as if you are seeing them for the first time, or indeed, as if you are seeing them for the last time, and you will see them with new eyes.

This practice of paying attention to the details of physical reality will also help with your holistic visualisation, helping to expand your imagination and your visual ability whilst grounding and framing your visualisation practice in physical reality.

When wanting to generate new ideas or to create solutions, cultivate the habit of thinking about the situations in images rather than in words. Images contain more information than the linear language of words. In fact, the latest scientific research seems to indicate that the information that is stored in our body's cells is composed of images. Because of the multi-layered language of symbolism, an image can contain a multiplicity of meanings and this way of storing information is more compact and takes up less energy than remembering information via the word.

So how do we activate our Inner Genie on purpose? One way is to slow down the frequency of our brainwaves so that they vibrate at what scientists call the Alpha frequency.

Brain Power

Remember those mirror neurons from the Storehouse of Knowledge that help us to learn, imitate, discern and understand social behaviour and interpret body language?

Well, our brain is made up of about 100 billion other types of neurons. Neurons function by firing energy and then resting. The number of times that neurons fire energy and rest per second is known as the brainwave frequency.

Neurons pulsate at their slowest during deep sleep and at their fastest when we are alert, awake or stressed.

Beta - 14 – 20 cycles per second – This is when your mind is focused in the Dimension of the Present Moment, on your outer senses and on what is going on around you, within the confines of time and space.

Alpha - 7 – 14 cycles per second – It is relatively easy to slip into the alpha state when we are daydreaming or listening to relaxing music. At the Alpha level, we may be awake or we may be asleep. But we are not engaged in the physical world and we don't have a sense of linear time. In the Alpha state, we can come up with new ideas, solve problems and create projects. We can work with guided imagery, the inner voice or experience inspiration.

Theta - 4 – 7 cycles per second – This is an even deeper subjective state. It is difficult to stay awake when your brain is vibrating so slowly. Advanced meditators are able to remain awake and alert at this level of the mind. It is possible to listen to audio recordings that contain binaural beats that guide the brain into the Theta state while you remain awake. Inspiration and ideas at this level comes mostly during the sleep state for people who do not meditate.

Delta - Below 4 cycles per second – This is when the mind enters the deepest level of sleep. Not much, if anything, can be remembered after being at the Delta level of the mind.

So the two levels that we can activate when we are looking for clarity, guidance, information, inspiration and creativity are the Alpha and Theta levels of the mind. At these levels, the brainwaves are not pulsating so fast that you're in a state of stress and they are not pulsating so slowly that you enter a state of deep dreamless sleep.

Sleep, meditation and prayer are all routes to connecting with the superconscious.

If meditation is not your bag or you don't perceive yourself as being a spiritual or religious person, then use the mechanism of natural sleep (unaided by drugs or sedatives) to communicate with your superconscious.

"To Sleep Perchance to Dream"

Before you go to sleep, give yourself an instruction that you will remember your dreams when you awaken. Then mentally ask your Inner Genie to communicate with you while you sleep. You may wish to ask for inspiration, guidance, solutions to problems or information.

We spend 20% of our sleep time dreaming so it is a productive use of our time to put our unconscious to work on solving problems and obstacles while we are asleep.

Our minds and bodies are not inactive while we sleep. Our hearts continue to beat and we continue to breathe. Our body is busy doing important work while we sleep - healing, repairing and renewing the body at a cellular, chemical and psychological level. Many of the self-healing functions that the body performs can only be carried out while the conscious mind is at rest. So although our focus is completely removed from the Dimension of the Present Moment when we sleep, everything else is still operating, including our minds.

Dreams have the power to program our waking lives for good or for ill whether we remember them or not. Our sleeping patterns affect the chemicals in our brain which, in turn, influences our moods. This, in turn, impacts how we interact with others, our behaviour and mindset and what we manifest. So it is a good idea to generate positive or constructive dreams.

Sleep-Dream cycles last for about 90 minutes.

The most vivid dreaming period occurs during the stage called REM sleep (Rapid Eye Movement sleep) which is similar to the Alpha state. Although our eyes are closed, the way they move is similar to the way our eyes move when we are watching a movie when awake.

In your first sleep cycle of 90 minutes, you may only spend five minutes dreaming. In the second sleep cycle, you may have a dream lasting about ten minutes. By the time, you arrive at your fifth sleep cycle, you may have a dream that lasts about 30 to 45 minutes.

In the morning before you wake up, you may have just experienced your last sleep cycle and the longest period of dreaming. Because the dreams we receive are not linear and not confined by time and space, they can appear jumbled and confusing to the conscious mind.

Even if your dreams don't make immediate sense, make notes about what you have dreamt as soon as you wake up.

Jot down phrases rather than full sentences describing the images and words that you remember. They may make sense immediately or nothing may come to you until later on.

Dream symbols and images can be personal to you or they can be transpersonal originating from the collective psyche of the human community. These symbols and visuals include iconic, mythical or religious imagery. Dream visuals from this source may also include racial imagery relating to your ancestry, ethnicity or nationality.

Use a process of free association of ideas and thoughts to interpret your dreams rather than looking up the meanings of symbols in a standardised dream therapy or dream reference book. You may also interpret all the different characters that appear in your dream as different aspects of yourself.

To generate a dream to gain inspiration, eliminate a creative block or solve a problem, as you lie in bed, right before you go to sleep, say to yourself: "I intend to have a dream that will give me guidance about [*your idea/goal/problem*] and I intend to remember and understand this information."

Even if you don't remember your dreams, the information will still be fed to your conscious mind during the course of the following day, and you will arrive at a solution or the idea will pop into your head. In fact, when it happens this way, it is sometimes more beneficial than having to decipher messages from a dream.

Meditation

If you have difficulty falling asleep or staying asleep, (one of the first signs of stress), then meditation would be the recommended way to access your Inner Genie as the journey to meditation is the same as the road to sleep.

Contrary to what many people think, meditation is not a withdrawal from the world. In fact, during this period of contemplation, your senses can be heightened. It can be, however, a withdrawal from the dimension of time.

Speaking of time, meditation doesn't have to take up hours of yours. There are many ways to contact the superconscious without being an advanced meditator (which can take years of practice). For instance, you can use guided meditations or the Holosync CDs. You can listen to recordings that contain Alpha and Theta beats to help guide you into a state of deep meditation.

The process is the same as for sleep. You set your intention, state what you wish to know or get clarity about. Forget about it and then meditate.

Don't expect answers to come immediately during meditation – but if it does, that's a bonus.

Our minds need to be still and quiet in order to listen and understand these messages clearly. Listening to these messages on a daily basis can help us to avoid or surmount setbacks, delays and obstacles, speeding up the journey of manifestation.

We can tap into this form of Intuitive Intelligence through deep physical relaxation of the body or meditation (deep relaxation of the mind).

As we live in the Age of Distraction and Information Overload, you may find it easier to contact Intuitive Intelligence through relaxation of the physical body rather than attempting to empty your mind which can be quite frustrating and therefore counterproductive.

But curiously enough, when your body is deeply relaxed, your mind begins to empty itself of its own accord.

A Simple Way to Meditate

This is a simple method of meditating which also incorporates self-hypnosis or autogenic conditioning.

Practise this exercise in a safe, quiet environment where you will be uninterrupted.

Make sure that you know the purpose of your meditation practice before you begin. Ascertain whether you are looking for guidance, inspiration, information, ideas or solutions. Alternatively, your purpose may be to set an intention for the future or programme a new positive behaviour or habit.

Make sure you focus on only one purpose for each meditation session.

Stage 1 – Relax the body

The first stage is to get yourself physically comfortable and relaxed using a process called fractional or progressive relaxation.

This involves intentionally relaxing a small section of the body at a time (such as a muscle), rather than attempting to relax the whole body at once. The gradual process of the exercise creates a state of deep relaxation.

You start with your feet, ankles and legs and then gradually move up the body, relaxing each part in turn.

You may wish to tighten each muscle and then release it gently in order to enhance the feeling of relaxation and release.

When you focus on a muscle or a small section of the body, you may wish to imagine it being filled with a healing blue or green light or energy field.

This first physical relaxation stage can take about from five to fifteen minutes depending on how tense you may be feeling.

Stage 2 – Relaxation of the Mind

After you have moved through the body, tensing and releasing each muscle in turn, use a mantra, phrase or chant to help your mind to enter a deep state of relaxation.

Popular mantras or chants include "OOOOOMMMMMMMMMMMMM...." This sound creates a healing vibration in the body.

Alternatively you can inhale with the word "so" and exhale with the word "hum".

Or you can chant "Hmmm" three times after each exhalation of breath.

If the idea of chanting makes you squirm, you may say the mantras in your mind only. Or if you prefer, you can focus silently on a positive word such as "LOVE" or "PEACE".

If you are a visual person (or rather, clairvoyant!), you may prefer to picture images that represent universal and humanitarian love (as opposed to familial and romantic love where challenging relationship issues can sometimes get in the

153

way of generating a peaceful mind). You may wish to picture a being that, for you, represents love, such as an angel or deity.

If you don't believe in angels or deities, then visualising ocean waves, water or white, blue or green light can also help at this stage.

This stage may take about ten to fifteen minutes.

Stage 3 - Hypnosis

When your mind is relaxed, you can enter the hypnotic state of consciousness.

To do so, picture yourself going slowly down a staircase counting backwards from ten to one with each step down that you take.

You can also picture yourself descending in a lift or elevator from the tenth floor to the basement.

Stage 4 – Make a Request or Set Your Intention

Once you have entered the hypnotic state (or the basement), you can:

(i)	set an intention
(ii)	program yourself with new thoughts or instructions for new positive behaviours
(iii)	ask your superconscious for guidance, ideas or information.

Remain at this level of the mind for ten to fifteen minutes in silence.

To disconnect from this level of the mind, picture yourself ascending the staircase counting from one to ten. When you reach the number ten, open your eyes.

Stage 5 - Grounding

This stage is very important. Write down any impressions, information, images, associations, insights or ideas that you received while you were in a state of altered consciousness when they are fresh in your mind.

154

Prayer

Prayer is another route to communicating with the superconscious.

You don't have to belong to a particular religion to pray or to connect to the Spiritual Source within you.

For many people, their definition of prayer is talking to the God of their understanding. However that is only one half of the prayer process. The crucial part which a lot of people miss out is listening for the reply.

Prayer is not a one way street. It is a two way process. So if and when you pray, be alert to Synchronicity, because this is the God of your Understanding answering you back.

You may receive the response in your own mind, using your own words, your own ways of expressing yourself or your own vocabulary (if you are clairaudient.)

You may also experience an answer through serendipity–through reading an article or book or through advice from an acquaintance.

Channelling

Some people write a letter to God and then write another letter in reply from the point of view of God.

In doing this, they find that they are able to spontaneously contact their Higher Self or Infinite Intelligence.

If you are not comfortable with the God Concept, you may prefer to imagine that the Universe is replying to your letter instead, or, if you prefer, you may write your answer as if the reply is coming from a wise figure from mythology.

The point of the exercise is to use your imagination to contact your Inner Genie and as part of the exercise or role play, part of your mind will take on the guise of an all knowing, wise and compassionate figure that has all the answers.

Imagination is but one doorway to genius. It is not an enemy or adversary to wisdom or knowledge.

Counsellors, Guides and Intuitive Companions

You can go further by personifying your Inner Genie and creating a character. Use your imagination and allow that figure to communicate with you using the language of your unconscious.

The word 'persona' is derived from Latin and literally means mask. *Persona* in Latin could mean false face or an assumed character, as in an actor in a play. Our personas or surface personalities are masks that we can put on or discard.

Nerdy skinny schoolboy Peter Parker becomes the Amazing Spiderman. The self-deprecating, clumsy journalist Clark Kent becomes Superman and the womanising bat-phobic playboy Bruce Wayne becomes the crime-fighting Batman. These fictional characters can change their identity just by donning a ridiculous costume or a mask.

You too can create an inner alter-ego who is your own adviser and superhero.

You may wish to create both a female and a male character to deal with different types of situations. These would represent the yin and yang aspects of your consciousness.

Some may be wary of these types of exercises in imagination seeing it as a road to craziness and delusion rather than a creative or fun way of thinking their way through obstacles, gaining clarity or receiving insights.

But with the correct and grounded approach, characterising this wise part of yourself is just a creative device, a tool for communicating with the deeper recesses of your mind. Creating a character to personify wisdom may help you to relate more easily to that deeper hidden part of yourself.

If any of these figures that your imagination conjures up uses language that is abusive or negative or egotistical, then the message is coming from the Home of the Shadow Self and the Wounded Child and not the Inner Genie. This is why it is important to work on strengthening your self-image and self-concept so that it is unshakable in the face of dissenting voices both from within (your shadow self) and without (doubting friends, family members and acquaintances).

Any negative language that you receive would refer to your own beliefs about yourself or the dysfunctional beliefs that other people might harbour about you. It is not to be treated as valid.

You would only want to contact the Home of the Shadow Self as a route to emotional healing.

Simple ways to connect to your Inner Genie

If the above suggestions seem too off-the-wall for you, here are some simpler ways that we can connect with our Inner Genie and in so doing, activate our potential for genius.

Physical exercise

Vigorous physical exercise releases endorphins that give you a feeling of well-being and rejuvenation. While focusing on exercising the physical body, the mind tends to empty itself without effort because we are focused in the present moment and on what the body is doing. Vigorous exercise has been found to reset or balance out our emotions.

Nature

Our minds work better when we are close to nature because we are a part of nature.

Being in natural beautiful surroundings outdoors can create an expansion of consciousness and well-being.

If you live in an urban area, listening to natural environmental sounds on a recording such as ocean waves, wind and animal sounds can also help to stimulate your connection to your superconscious.

Classical music

Some forms of music tend to overstimulate the nervous system. But classical music tends to have a holistically beneficial effect on the whole person because of its organised structures and rhythms. It is one of the highest forms of restoration and rejuvenation because the holes in our vertebrae each resonate to different notes on the music scale. In fact, if you rest small portable pillow speakers or similar halfway between the navel and your pubic bone and play classical music into it, it has the power to uplift, de-stress and take you into the Alpha state.

Silence

Entering into a session of silence and stillness for 30 to 60 minutes, depending on how long you can do it without your mind wandering – is another way to contact the Inner Genie. During this period, you don't read, write or listen to music. Solutions, ideas and insights arrive once your mind sits still. Paradoxically, when you feel the most pressured and time-starved, then that is the time that you need to enter a period of silence and stillness.

Eleven

The Team's Spirit

You may have heard the old joke about the faith of a man dangling off the edge of a cliff. Here is another variation of the tale.

There was once a man enjoying an afternoon stroll when he suddenly fell off the edge of a cliff. He managed to cling on to the edge of the precipice with his legs dangling above the deep crevice below. But the man was not afraid for he had faith that the Lord would save him from death.

Moments later, an off-duty firefighter came along and saw the man dangling off the edge of the cliff. "Don't worry mate, I'll call the rest of my brigade and we'll rescue you!" he shouted down.

"No need!" said the man. "No need! I am trusting in the Lord to save me and He will!"

The firefighter shrugged and went on his way.

Then a chap who volunteered on the weekends as part of a mountain rescue team caught sight of the fellow clinging dangerously off the precipice. "Don't worry!" he shouted. "I can call on the rest of my team to help you!"

"No need!" replied the man. "No need! I am trusting in the Lord to save me and He will!"

The volunteer shook his head but went on his way.

Then a man on holiday from his native Samaria came upon the fellow dangling off the edge of the cliff and said, "Hang on! I will climb down and rescue you and patch you up!"

"No need!" said the man. "No need! I am trusting in the Lord to save me and He will!"

159

The Good Samaritan went away reluctantly. A few minutes later, the man fell off the edge of the cliff and died.

When he arrived in heaven, he said plaintively to the Lord, "Nice to meet you and all that but I trusted in you to save me and you didn't! Why not?"

And the Lord said, "What do you mean I didn't help you? I sent you a firefighter, a mountain rescue man and even a Good Samaritan and you turned them all down!"

"But I was expecting *you* to save me!" the man said, in disappointment.

"My dear fellow," said the Lord. "You prayed and your prayers were answered. For it is through the help, support and encouragement of other human beings that I make my Presence known."

Whatever we want to manifest, be it a goal, dream, project, vision, creative endeavour, piece of art, charity or business – it cannot exist in isolation and we cannot accomplish it alone. Somewhere along the way, we are going to need other people whether it is in the capacity of collaborators, partners, clients, coaches, teachers, trainers, students, readers, mentors or recipients of our services.

The goals that we choose to manifest may ultimately be for our own self-fulfilment, but at the same time, they must exist in a wider context. A writer needs readers, a teacher needs students, a therapist needs clients, a business needs customers and works of art needs witnesses or an audience.

We therefore need to tap into the resources provided by the Psyche of the Human Community.

In Chapter Nine, we looked at the Psyche of the Human Community, only in its context as a dimension of the mind.

The Psyche of the Human Community was described as the home of ideas, inventions, philosophies, prejudices, collective fears and phobias, religious attitudes and also as the part of the mind that is influenced by advertising, propaganda and subliminal imagery.

But the Psyche of the Human Community can also have a much more conscious practical influence in our daily lives.

Tollan

Tollan was a legendary city in Mexico during the Aztec era, the name meaning "Place of Many Neighbourhoods". It was a centre or arts and crafts, palaces and gold. The historical existence of Tollan was doubted by scholars until archaeological discoveries were made at the end of the nineteenth century.

The collective human mind has its own kind of Tollan. Within this legendary city of the mind, there are several realms, or if you like, neighbourhoods: communities nested within communities.

Although there may be some overlap between these communities, I have identified these categories broadly as:

1. The Realm of Ancestral Memory
2. The Plane of Popular Culture
3. The Collective DreamScape
4. Our Ethnic and National Heritage
5. Our Social Identity
6. Collective Intelligence

We all have access to the Realm of Ancestral Memory. We may not remember the actual historical events or the things that happened to our ancestors consciously. But our cellular and genetic memories possess knowledge of things that we may have no conscious awareness of.

The Plane of Popular Culture is the home of trends, changes in spoken language and changes in ways of communication, movies, music and celebrity obsession. From the Plane of Popular Culture, we receive the kind of information that can seep into our minds via a weird kind of cultural osmosis. At its most superficial, this plane provides the watercooler moments. It is the terrain of gossip.

The Plane of Popular Culture is both organic and manufactured. Therefore it also includes the imagery, concepts, icons and ideas that are birthed by the three groups that influence our hearts and our minds: the media, politics and religion.

We all have a personal dreamscape generated by images stored in the Home of the Shadow Self and the Storehouse of Knowledge. But we also have a Collective DreamScape formed by images from our universal ancestral memory as well as the images that are fed into our minds every day through advertising, movies and other forms of popular culture. Therefore when we sleep, our dreams are populated with images and information from both our personal and Collective DreamScape.

We are also influenced by our ethnic, national or sociocultural heritage. For some people, like myself, our ethnicity may be different from our nationality and our social class may also have an additional part to play in the mix. Thus we may belong to several diverse social communities, each having a different self-concept, self-image and shadow.

A miniature collective psyche group can become formed around racial or gender identity, our age or generation, our political affiliations, our value system, religion, occupation, social class and even (or especially) gang culture. Each mini group would have a collective self-image, self-concept and shadow which would form the collective spirit of the group – the Team's Spirit.

Reflective Questions

Who do I identify as being my most dominant group? In other words, which sector of the population do I feel the most kinship with or have the strongest bond with psychologically? (This could be in relation to your family, your race, gender, age, occupation, aspirations, hobbies/interests and so on).

If you don't feel as if you belong to any particular group, then answer the questions below using the "whole of humankind" as your dominant group.

What is my current role in my dominant group? What is my present contribution?

Does my goal for self-fulfilment and manifestation intersect or connect with the destiny or fulfilment or highest good of my dominant group?

What do I have to offer this group through my skills, gifts, insights, life experiences and personality?

How can I shape our collective future?

Can you imagine your group at its highest, most ideal level? Can you envision the Entelechy, Collective Essential Self or the Common Evolution of the group that you most identify with? Does a representative image or symbolic logo spring to mind?

Collective Intelligence

There is also a spiritual dimension within the Psyche of the Human Community. For some people, this collective spiritual dimension of the mind takes on the form of a vast metaphorical library or body of knowledge. Others may refer to this part of the mind as collective wisdom, collective intelligence, collective consciousness or group resonance. This part of the Human Psyche contains the race's highest potential.

In Chapter 45 of *the Aquarian Gospel of Jesus the Christ,* Jesus is travelling in Greece and someone asks him whether the voice of the Delphic Oracle belongs to an angel, man or God.

Jesus replies that the voice of the Oracle is the voice of the collective wisdom of Delphi. He refers to this Voice as a giant mind, a living soul that has the capacity to think, hear and speak: a soul that is nourished by the collective wisdom and masterminds of Delphi.

Similarly at its highest, most spiritual level, the Psyche of the Human Community is a giant mind. It is a living soul that is fed by our most noble and wise thoughts, morals, values, ideas, gifts, talents and philosophies.

In Napoleon Hill's famous book *Think and Grow Rich,* he describes his nightly practice of having various figures of history spring from his imagination and come to life to discuss his daily life issues around a table with him giving him advice, pointers and guidance.

You may want to carry out a similar exercise. Which iconic figures do you admire? Mahatma Gandhi, JFK, Mother Teresa or Martin Luther King? Could you invite any of these people to an imaginary summit at your Round Table?

You may prefer to create a cast of fictional inner genies who are guest experts in your fields and endeavours of interest.

These experts would be aspects of the collective mastermind but these subjective creations would be *super*personalities rather than the subpersonalities that are formed unconsciously as a childhood reaction to the way that others treat us.

Again, it has to be stressed that these exercises are not to be taken literally. These are exercises in imagination to help us to access inner wisdom more easily. It may or may not be a spiritual experience for you. But it is a vehicle by which your own superconscious can communicate to you wearing different clothes and by using the tools of the imagination and the workshop of the mind.

Humanity's Shadow

Just as we have a collective higher consciousness, we also have a collective shadow.

Humanity has a dark side that is rooted in fear. Individuals within a group can have a self-image that doesn't result in the best outcome for them, a small sense of self that holds them back or an inflated exaggerated sense of self that creates paranoia, insecurity and fear.

When one mind or voice unites with other like-minded parts of the human consciousness, it can either create a climate of fear and insecurity or a choir of empowerment and enlightenment, depending on the mindsets of the people within the group. Most groups create a climate that falls somewhere between these two ends of the spectrum.

You can go on a spiritual retreat or a lovely holiday out in the country and feel revitalised, refreshed, as if all is well in the world and totally blissed out. Then as soon as you return to the "rat-race" – otherwise known as the human race – you can get sucked back into your habitual way of thinking, talking, behaving and being – not out of weakness or laziness, but out of the immense power of WE. For such is the mammoth power of the collective group, or to bring it down to biology, the power of our mirror neurons.

It can prove to be a colossal challenge to transform yourself when the people that you spend most of your time with are deeply entrenched in the ways of being and behaviour that you desire to move away from.

One way of dealing with this challenge is to find a way of leaving your dominant group environment or, if this is not practical, to find ways of associating and networking and bringing new people into your life who have like-minded aspirations.

Another way of dealing with belonging to a group with a toxic or negative mindset is to generate change from within the "belly of the beast" by forming your own empowering miniature group and leading by example.

As an aside, although this is not a book about changing the world, there is little point in changing yourself and finding your authentic path in life if you live in an environment that is inherently diseased (i.e. a society that lives from a fear or hate-based perspective).

There have been many people in history that have tuned into the collective shadow of the human psyche in an attempt to wield immense power and gain success. The Nazi movement is one such example. A BBC TV documentary series entitled *The*

Dark Charisma of Adolf Hitler explores how Hitler was able to engender a kind of love-worship akin to religious fervour in his followers whilst preaching a doctrine and philosophy of hate, racialism and paranoia.

Tuning into the collective shadow and manipulating the psyche of the human community by stimulating their fears has led to war, genocide and all-round general disaster and tragedy in human history.

For the purposes of manifesting your dreams and goals, you need to tune into the "highest" part of the Human Psyche: the realm of Collective Wisdom and Intelligence which is based on collaboration rather than manipulation.

> *What is reality anyway? Nothing but a collective hunch.*
> Lily Tomlin

We can tap into the "higher" resources of the human community at a conscious external level.

It is a two-way street which involves attracting the people that we need to help us realise our fullest potential as well as having our own innate authentic power and positive influence over others. We attract not only the people that can help us but also people that we in turn can help. We help these people by creating value for them whether it is by providing information or services, through our expertise, our craft, or through the wisdom bestowed upon us by life experience.

This system of "paying it forward", this synergistic energy exchange can engender great manifestation results. The effects of your manifestation practice will be multiplied and accelerated when you work in collaboration with others tapping into the power of group consciousness.

We often bond and form groups through a shared sense of victimhood. In forming your new partnerships, networks and relationships, avoid bonding with other people through a narrative of victimhood or complaints. Resist the temptation to validate each other's miseries, setbacks and tales of woe. Instead form your group around the perspective of

166

empowerment so that you can generate solutions to transcend problems, obstacles, disappointments and setbacks.

There is a place for that kind of support where your needs, your story, your tragedies or your traumas are validated and heard by a therapeutic group. The main purpose of these groups is to create a space for healing old physical, emotional and spiritual wounds. But for the purposes of manifestation and transformation, join or form groups that are based around creating an environment for the shared growth and development of its members.

These "power circles" should not be about reinforcing and encouraging each other's negative self-images or fostering a sense of helplessness in the face of "Fate". Nor should it involve bitching about people in other social or cultural groups. Feedback should be constructive and helpful rather than crushingly critical. Your empowering micro-group should be free of judgement and be a place of psychological safety.

There are many different ways or levels of connecting with the collective human psyche to aid you with your manifestation practice.

You already belong to a network which is composed of everybody that you know from your casual acquaintances to close friends, colleagues, relatives and even the tenuous links with people that you have met once or twice. Forming a network is one way of generating your own web of synchronicity where unlikely connections can spring up and link you to potential opportunities.

You may wish to take an active role in connecting or introducing people you know to other contacts. Work out how the people you know can assist each other according to their own particular gifts, skills and knowledge. Generate relevant connections related to their hobbies, interests, outlook and skills. Create your own bank or pool of people/experts, your own referral system and resources that you can draw upon.

Members of your network will repay you in kind and introduce you to other individuals who can help you out. Sometimes the process may not be reciprocal. Maybe you won't receive help from the same person that you helped but you will receive help from another direction.

Nowadays you can create your Network virtually on the internet via Facebook, Twitter and so forth.

At a deeper level, you may be interested in joining or forming a Mastermind group. This is a more tightly focused group than your network. Your Mastermind would be a small group of success-minded people (say a group of five to ten) that you meet on a regular basis –once a week, fortnight or month – virtually or in person. They would be a group of like-minded people that you can trust and with whom you can share your aspirations and challenges. You will need to set up a few ground rules or key agreements beforehand so that the focus of the group remains positive, success-orientated and focused on aspiration, support and motivation.

You may prefer or find it easier to create a success-orientated partnership through a Buddy. You would check in with your buddy on a daily basis or maybe a couple of times a week, updating each other on your progress, brainstorming ideas and coming up with solutions to problems. You would both be working at the same level, supporting each other and holding each other accountable to the goals and intentions that you set. As you would be working in tandem with your buddy, it would be different from a coaching/mentor relationship. The image of a see-saw springs to mind.

Coaches and mentors or experts who will take you under their wing are another external resource of the collective human psyche. You may wish to consult with an expert in personal development or in the area where you want to succeed. Experts and mentors will point out to you where you need to progress, what you need to work on, what is stopping you, what you can change, what you can improve and help you to hone your gifts and cultivate your strengths.

You can choose to receive further formal education and training. You can learn from the masters in your field, working with consultants in your area of specialisation.

On a more informal level, you can read the biographies and autobiographies of people who have succeeded in the area that you want to succeed in. You can invest in audio programmes relevant to your area of interest (if applicable) that you can listen to while you commute, travel or relax.

Whether you draw upon the resources of a coach, a mastermind group or your social network, you want to cultivate relationships with people who will stretch you, who won't cut you down and who don't suffer from Tall Poppy Syndrome.

You will be both a teacher and a student allowing others to complement what you have to offer, working in collaboration with them and sharing your vision.

When you are assembling a team of helpers or recruiting assistants or co-workers, you don't want to select a bunch of clones who are exactly like you with the same skillset. But you *do* want to select people who share the same mindset as you and who will help you to form a collective Team Spirit that is empowering and forward-moving.

An individual may be really skilled and excellent at what they do, they may even be the best in the business, but if their mindset is at odds with yours, it could bring the energy or consciousness of the group down.

You will need to recruit people who can complement your weaknesses, who are skilled and experienced in the areas where you may have lesser knowledge. But you will also be gifted in areas where they may be under-experienced and so your mutual gifts will help to elevate each other so it would not be a one-way or imbalanced relationship.

Setting out the context and shared concrete agreements and principles about the spirit, mindset and purpose of your team at the outset of your endeavour will prevent misunderstandings and conflicts later on.

Be sure to let the people in your team know how much you appreciate and value their contribution either through your actions or your words. Sometimes people don't realise how grateful we are for their input and contribution unless we let them know overtly and directly.

169

Chopsticks

When we want to influence others, we often need to practice what we preach but without making it look like too much hard work or like a heavy-duty obligation. Through our behaviour, we lead by example and model the behaviour and the way that we prefer that other people do things for us. Another way to influence others is to explain the consequences and drawbacks of not doing what has been agreed upon, as well as explaining the benefits and what is in it for them.

You may prefer to create a group where leadership is relationship-orientated rather than hierarchical, a group that is organic, syncretic and playful in nature.

If you have difficulties in connecting with others, you may need to examine your beliefs about collaboration, competition and how safe you feel about trusting other people.

There are many variations of the parable about the difference between heaven and hell. I have heard a Korean version and a Vietnamese version. I also heard another version in the film, *The Wisdom of Crocodiles* described as a dream of Confucius. There may be other versions of the same tale. But here, in essence, is the story of the difference between heaven and hell:

Hell is a luxurious place with a banquet of delicious food filled with people dressed in the finest clothes. However in hell, the people are starving. They can't eat the food in front of them because they are unable to use the giant chopsticks that have been provided for them to use to eat the food.

Heaven is a luxurious place with a banquet of delicious food filled with people dressed in the finest clothes. They cannot feed themselves with the giant chopsticks that have been provided for them. But they are not starving. They are laughing and smiling. Because they have learnt how to use the chopsticks to feed each other.

Twelve

The World Wide Web

You may have heard the *other* joke about a man dangling off the edge of a cliff. Here is another variation of it.

There was once a man taking an afternoon walk on a windy day when suddenly the wind blew him off the edge of a cliff.

"HELP! Is there anybody up there that can help me?" he shouted, as he clung on for dear life.

To his surprise, God Himself replied saying, "I can help you. But do you trust me?"

"Of course I do!" replied the man. "Please hurry!"

"Just follow my instructions," said God. "And you'll be safe. Understand?"

"Yes!" shouted back the man.

"All you have to do is let go," said God. "And then I will catch you."

The man paused to think this over. Then he called out again, "Is there anybody *else* up there that can help me?"

"We're all having a bad time...it's called life!"
Coronation Street

We are all connected to a Spiritual and Creative Life Force. We may choose to view this Force as a specific religious deity within a theological system, or as Universal Energy. Others may choose to see this Force as a psychological concept or as a part of Nature.

171

There are many factors that can stop us from connecting with or believing in this Creative Life Force.

One factor is a strong belief in the idea of Fate, in the notion that our destiny is predetermined and cannot be changed.

Another belief is that punishments are being visited upon us by God for past transgressions in this or previous lifetimes.

When we are beset by obstacles, delays, disappointments, tragedies or destruction, life can seem very dark. Ugly or tragic things do happen such as heinous crimes, physical and psychological abuse, betrayal, the loss of a job, the loss of one's home, the loss of a spouse or the loss of a child.

These sorts of events can lead us to believe that rather than being supported by the Universe, Life itself is out to get us. The Universe is seen as a great big tease out to torment, taunt and tantalise us with dreams of success and hopes that can never be realised. A fatalistic attitude or believing that certain things aren't meant to be can lead us to become passive observers of existence rather than active co-creators of Life. We give up, believing that the way things are, is the way that things will always be.

We say things half in jest like: "Somebody up there doesn't like me" or "I must have done something terrible in a former life" – when beset by problem followed by crisis followed by calamity followed by misfortune. It is reminiscent of the saying about the light at the end of the tunnel being an oncoming train about to mow you down.

It can be a challenge to perceive the Divine Order behind the apparent chaos that we call Life.

Some people who believe in the Law of Attraction may believe that their thoughts and beliefs invited these dark events into their lives. But Life is not as simplistic as that. A distinction needs to be drawn.

There are the events that we attract into our lives through negative thinking and disempowering beliefs.

But there are also the seemingly dark events that happen because of the cycles of Nature, life and human experience that

172

are nothing to do with blame or the fault or the thoughts of the individual. And as teachers or therapists often say, even though what happens to us may not be our fault, it is *our responsibility* to transcend and overcome the obstacles that fall into our path through the power of positive believing, holistic visioning, releasing the past, setting intentions for the future and connecting with the greater all-encompassing power that is Life itself.

Life can be dark but as the Reverend Michael Beckwith teaches, the dark is where things can develop, like images in a dark room, in the darkest hours before the dawn, we can sow seeds of new opportunity.

Often we mistake comfort for happiness and things can get stale. When we hit rock bottom, when circumstances change our life seemingly for the worse, we can use the disaster as a catalyst or as an opportunity for growth.

We all have experiences in life that hold the possibility of teaching us compassion, empathy and that can lead us to our purpose and contribution. Transcending something horrible that happened to us may lead us to a vocation where we help others going through a similar experience to get over and transcend their pain.

If you believe that your soul's destiny predates your birth or this lifetime, you may also believe that each life experience is a teacher that is leading you towards your greater destiny.

Some New Age/modern spiritual practices involve covering over the dark cracks with a thin spiritual veneer of denial of the bad things that can happen in life.

But bad things do happen and often with the perspective of Time, we see how going through one dark experience meant that we were led to meeting someone significant in our life, or how losing a job led to us starting a business or how an emotional childhood crisis led to helping children as a career in adulthood. While the experience was happening, it may have felt like the end of the world, but when you reached the other side of the tunnel, you survived, you got out of it, you coped and you transcended it.

Tragedy, obstacles and trauma have often spurred people on to scientific discovery, to producing great works of art or to composing musical masterpieces that have benefited or enriched others well beyond the span of the originators' own lifetime.

The Creative Life Force

The Creative Life Force is an Energetic Field of opportunity and synchronicity. This Energetic Field can also be activated inside of us. When we are connected to this Source, when we are plugged in, things become effortless and opportunities appear seemingly spontaneously. Chance meetings, surprise encounters and unexpected turns can propel us into different directions and new avenues.

This Creative Energetic Field has been given many names within different world cultures, religions and science.

In Buddhism, there is the "net" of the god Indra that binds the universe together.

In the Hopi story of how the universe began, the world emerged via a web weaved by "Spider Grandmother". This web was the *great connector* which linked all things and beings in the world together.

Nowadays the words "web" and "net" are used in a different context but with the same idea behind it: that of the InterNET which has turned the world into a global village. Using the same analogy, we can also view the powerful Energetic Field as a kind of internet or inter-network or indeed INNER NETWORK.

Another word for the energetic field which also has connotations with computer networks is ETHER. Ether (or aether) is the word that the Ancient Greeks used to describe the Energetic Field which was seen as the space between everything. It can be translated as "pure fresh air", "upper region of the atmosphere" or "sky". In Greek mythology, Aether was the first-born elemental god of light or of the upper air of heaven.

Some cultures call this field of energy *"prana"* which can be translated as *life force, vitality* or *breath.* Other cultures refer to this energy as *"chi"* or *"ki"* and others refer to it as the *Holy Spirit* or the *Holy Breath.*

The philosopher Plato called it the World Soul (*anima mundi*).

Indian scriptures (the *Rig Veda*) speak of a FORCE that was present before Time began. They call the Force *Brahman* or the Unborn god that holds the whole universe together. Everything that exists emerges from this Potential. Everything that becomes manifest is a different face of this "Unborn" force.

In the Seth books, the great psychic and writer Jane Roberts, when channelling the information from "Seth", referred to this Force as ALL THAT IS.

Some philosophers and teachers call it the Great Nest of Being.

The idea that we are connected to an underlying Source of Intelligence can also be viewed from a scientific perspective. Even though science may use a different vocabulary, it is still describing the same phenomenon in different terms.

Physicist and superstring theory expert, Michio Kaku calls this Force, the "Quantum Hologram".

When the physicist Max Planck accepted his Nobel Prize for his study of the atom, he said of the force which holds the atom together, "We must assume behind this force the existence of a conscious and intelligent mind. This mind is the matrix of all matter."

Albert Einstein is attributed as having said, "I see a pattern but my imagination cannot picture the maker of the pattern...we all dance to a mysterious tune intoned in the distance by an invisible piper."

Writer Gregg Braden calls the Energetic Field, "The Divine Matrix". He describes the Divine Matrix as being "everywhere all the time" and as an intelligent force that responds to human emotion.

Dr Wayne Dyer describes this force as the field of intention which he says has seven qualities: it is creative, loving, kind, abundant, beautiful, expansive and receptive.

So according to some branches of scientific thought and certain religions, mythologies and philosophies, this Creative Energetic Field is *omnipresent, omnipotent* and *omniscient.*

When we learn to tune ourselves into this Energetic Field, we draw the experiences, resources and people to us that we need and then we succeed – as if by magic.

This energetic field can also help to bring in new ideas and stimulate actions as well as instigate an effortless flow of events that can move you towards your goal.

Two to Tango – Dancing with the Universe

To develop the idea of enjoying the ride rather than rushing to get to the journey's end, we must do what some people call "dancing with the universe", working "hand-in-hand" as a co-creator with All That Is to manifest your dreams.

When you collaborate with the Creative Life Force, the universe capitalises on the actions you take and multiplies the results.

Mike Dooley teaches that for every little step you take, the Universe takes thousands of steps on your behalf to advance you in the direction of your dreams.

The German writer, Goethe said, "...the moment one definitely commits oneself, then Providence moves too. All sorts of things occur to help one that would never otherwise have occurred. A whole stream of events issues from the decision...which no man could have dreamed would have come his way."

Dancing with the universe can be a somewhat difficult juggling act. It can mean surrendering and going with the flow and following your intuition while taking strategic, logical, focused steps towards the accomplishment of your dream.

The Creative Life Force has a perpetual drive to create and to expand. Because we are made in the likeness of this Creative Life Force, we humans share the same instinct and impulse towards expansion. Therefore the Creative Field of Life is not only an Agent of Being, it is also an Agent of Becoming.

Creation is not a finite act that lasted six days : it is an ongoing process, a perpetual event. The Universe continues to evolve, to manifest and to co-create with all of life (including plants, animals, minerals and humanity). A new day is created every day with each sunrise and we have the option to make each day different from all the other days that preceded it.

Similarly we, as individuals, are not a finite act of creation. We continuously evolve from the embryo to infancy to childhood, adolescence and the various stages of adulthood. We, as individuals, are an infinite act of creation. We are a continual work-in-progress. We never stop evolving although we may try to resist change. This lifetime is just one chapter in one book in the Library of Our Soul.

It is our instinct to grow, develop, change, transform, age and evolve, just like the universe. When we don't evolve, we stagnate and then we wither.

We need to connect and align our life purposes with this divine creative instinct of the universe. In so doing, we not only create maximum results but we get a deep sense of fulfilment rather than the shallow and transient feeling of fairytale success with its fictional promise of "happy ever after" that follows an achievement.

The Creative Field of Life is an animating force. It can break itself down and rebuild itself – like energetic Lego. It is within everything and everyone. It is the substance from which we are formed, the basic building blocks of life on an energetic level – just as the cells are the basic building blocks of life on the physiological level.

All the potential inventions, products, ideas and unborn children already exist in this creative soup. They remain dormant, unexpressed, unrealised and unmanifested until a person or a partnership or a group tunes in and aligns with an idea, discovers the need for a product or invention, makes space in their life for that child or develops a solution for a problem that exists on the physical level.

Artists will express the Creative Life Force through works of art. Composers and musicians will express this Force through

177

music. Writers will express this Force through creating characters or writing articles, essays, books or poetry. Inventors will express this Creative Field through developing products and entrepreneurs through generating and commercialising ideas, services and products.

Every being is a unique manifestation of this Creative Life Force and everyone takes a slice of the Creative Life Pie and expresses it differently.

We are able to manifest to the degree that we are able to receive, attune and be receptive to what the Creative Life Force has to offer. Our ability to manifest is in direct correlation with our ability to listen, to be guided and to receive and also with our ability to act upon this guidance.

Manifestation is the art of making the invisible visible and the intangible tangible.

We are the vehicles through which the unexpressed, the still to be invented, the books yet to be written, the music yet to be composed, the art yet to be painted, the people yet to be born, become realised and become part of this physical reality. We are the agents of manifestation and the physical apparatus through which All That Is can express its ideas, its art, music, fashion, philosophies and inventions.

The Creative Life Force has a playful, fun aspect which rejoices in diversity, renewal and detail. Each act of creation is an act of joy and triumph on the part of this Creative Field. But the person that chooses to perform this act of creation may experience the throes of metaphorical childbirth and labour pains before their co-creation becomes fully manifest or even accepted and embraced by others.

This Creative Life Force has an innate intelligence which we all share. This innate intelligence is found in our ability to breathe, the way our bodies function and repair themselves or the things we do automatically without knowing how we do them such as the mechanics of walking, talking or driving.

We don't need to know the mechanics of how we do what we do in order to be able to do it. We don't need to know how electricity works in order to switch on a light. Similarly, we don't need to understand exactly how the Creative Life Force works in order to be able to use it for the manifestation of our goals.

In fact, if we possess too much certainty about the direction of our goals, we can close down other options and opportunities and keep ourselves limited. A certain level of specificity is required when creating a vision for a goal. However a degree of uncertainty and flexibility can leave room for growth, development, expansion and learning.

Connecting with the Creative Life Force

With holistic visualisation, we project what we want or we picture and imagine what we desire using our subjective inner senses. But with holistic visioning, we connect with the Creative Field of Life in order to be intuitively guided.

The Universe can behave like *Amazon.com* and deliver what you order according to your specifications. But when you connect with the Creative Life Force through listening rather than instructing, your creativity, your artistry, your vision and your mission becomes more authentic, more fulfilling and more rewarding and sometimes more expansive when fully realised.

Instead of giving commands to the Universe/God (for example like with the process of Cosmic Ordering), we ourselves receive instructions and guidance which leads to a deeper level of manifestation.

We can communicate with the Creative Field of Life through the language of emotions and our imagination.

It is like tuning into a particular radio frequency or channel. You get a better reception from the station when you are aligned with your Essential Self. You can hear and understand guidance more clearly. You receive insights much more clearly when you tune into the frequency of the Universal Field of Life through the perspective of your Essential Self and not through the perspective of your insecure, doubting Shadow Self whose self-image is made up of the opinion of others or whose identity is tied to a job title or a dominant characteristic or a relationship role.

179

You view your intention from the perspective of your Inner Genie or your Essential Self and then when you connect this intention with the Universal Field of Life, the manifestation wheel is set in motion.

When you connect with the Creative Field of Life, it is a somatic experience that you feel in the body rather than in the mind. It may be experienced as a gut instinct or as a feeling in your bones or in your heart energy.

This is a process whereby you are connecting with Consciousness itself. Consciousness precedes thought. Because thought follows consciousness, by using this process, you are automatically changing the pattern of your thoughts in a more positive and empowering direction. Your thoughts shape your beliefs and they influence your behaviour. Feminine power teachers Claire Zammit and Katherine Woodward-Thomas always say that our goals and desires manifest through who we are *being* rather than what we are doing.

When working on an intellectual or conceptual level to discover your next step or what you want, the mind can throw up a myriad choice of endless possibilities. But when you connect with the body, there is usually only one choice that the body resonates with at a particular time. There is usually only one choice that will give you that "Yes" feeling and provide the clarity that you need to make your next move.

Step by Step process

Connect with the Creative Life Force after sitting in silence for some minutes.

You may experience the energy through images, colours or feel it in your body or as a combination of all three sensory modes. Alternatively you may simply experience the Creative Life Force as peace.

State what you want to know, or where you need guidance, or what you need or desire, or simply state your intention for your highest and best future.

Connect with the Field in the way that is most comfortable and powerful for you.

Remain in the Silence for five to ten minutes experiencing the energy using your most dominant sense. For example, if you are a visual person, you will experience the Creative Life Force in your mind's eye as a colour, shape or image that surrounds you.

On the other hand, if you possess strong kinaesthetic senses, you may experience the Creative Life Force as sensations in your body or as emotions. Allow yourself to be receptive to the energy whether you experience it as pulsations, tingling, vibrations or floating.

As per usual with many of the practices in this book, you focus on your intention but not on the hows of the situation. Remain in the silence and experience the energy (be it visually, physically or through your auditory senses) for five to ten minutes.

The next stage of the process is to ask yourself:

What does the Universal Creative Field of Life want to express through me in my next step towards manifesting this goal?

Or:

What would this Primal Creative Force like to manifest through my particular set of skills, talents and gifts?

You may see images or words, feel emotions or sensations, receive insights or get ideas. This process doesn't have to take long – as little as five minutes up to about twenty minutes.

More answers, solutions and guidance will continue to come to you as you go about your daily life. As you implement your plans and take action, synchronicities, coincidences and opportunities will occur if you stay open to possibility and remain consciously connected to the Creative Force.

This practice can be used instead of, or together with, the practice of Holistic Visualisation outlined in Chapter Three.

(If you are doing both practices, then you would do them separately on alternate days. For example, you would do the visualisation technique on Monday and then the connection with the Life Force exercise on Tuesday).

An alternative method of this visioning practice is to use the letter writing technique by expressing the answers to the above questions in the form of a letter to yourself from the perspective and in the words of the Creative Universal Field of Life.

This chapter has contained concepts, ideas and practices that may seem somewhat obscure and esoteric but in the next and final chapter, we will conclude with the more straightforward concepts and practices of generating financial abundance.

Thirteen

Attracting Abundance

Financial Abundance

Although it *is* possible to be satisfied and happy without experiencing any great financial and material abundance, it is easier to thrive and focus on your purpose if you have one less thing to worry about.

Financial abundance gives us resources, the capacity to help others and the ability to make things happen. Financial hardship may create stress and distract us from the big picture, purpose or vision of our lives because we are too busy struggling to survive.

Once the basic fundamental needs in life such as food, shelter and clothing have been met, we then usually feel freer to focus our attention on self-actualisation, health and creating wealth.

An important part of Manifestation Psychology lies in developing a mindset of abundance. The ultimate goal of any long-term financial endeavour is not to be rich, but to be *enriched* psychologically as well as in the material sense.

If you are experiencing financial challenges or you believe that you are not earning up to your full potential, you may wish to learn about (or revise) the principles of attracting abundance.

This information comes at the end of this book rather than at the beginning so as to avoid money being our primary focus and motive for manifestation.

But why should we avoid making money our main manifestation focus? Because:

THERE IS NO MONEY IN MONEY

Money is an illusion. It is a symbol or a representation. It is a tool, currency, a language, a means of communication and the expression of an idea. But there is no inherent value, for example, in a fifty dollar bill or in a twenty pound note. The paper it is printed on is not worth anything in itself. There is no longer any correspondence between money and gold.

Money is not meaning*less* however. Rather it is a way of *creating* meaning, a way of expressing wealth or lack or debt.

There is, however, money in assets. There is money in the creation of something new or in the adaptation of something old into something new.

There is money in creating information, in manufacturing products, in offering services or in establishing systems that generate passive income.

But there is no actual money in money.

Money should be the means to an end, not an end in itself.

When practising holistic visualisation, don't picture the money that you need to get what you want or how much you need to earn. Instead think of the actual things that you would like to obtain or the actual things you will do in your desired job or lifestyle. Remember, there may be other routes to what you want, other means of getting there than via the Money Highway. Visualise what you would like to produce or create.

Forget the "Show me the money" philosophy. Chasing after money is like chasing after the wind whereas wealth is an energy pattern.

Someone once said that the only people that make money are the people that work in a mint. So shift the emphasis from "making money" to attracting and creating wealth.

Focus on developing and mastering skills that are transferable, adaptable and marketable.

Remember that *you are your greatest asset and resource.* Your skills, knowledge, life experience and ideas are the seeds of your future profits, productivity and wealth.

> *"Opportunity is missed by most people because it is dressed in overalls and looks like work."*
> Thomas Edison

Work is one of the main (if somewhat unpopular) paths to abundance.

There is great wisdom in beginning where you are right now and in the old adage," bloom where you are planted".

Perhaps your current day job is just a stopgap. Maybe your job is part of your back-up plan or a safety net. But it is still part of the journey towards abundance, part of the gestation period while you are creating or rediscovering your true livelihood.

Obviously working for an hourly wage or a fixed monthly salary will not lead to great riches, but it is a platform, a starting point, a means of security, while you create, plan and build. You may have to be a part-time creator while you work at a full-time job, until such time as your creative passion becomes your livelihood.

But everything is part of the plan. So if you are stuck in a mundane job with weird or flaky colleagues, what are you learning from being where you are now? Even if all the people you are meeting are "anti-teachers", that is, people who are teaching you about what you don't want to be or how you don't want to turn out, then that is still all useful information.

What experiences, knowledge, and skills are you acquiring in your present work that you can apply to cultivating your dream? Who are you meeting and networking with on a daily basis? What synchronicities and coincidences are occurring?

Learning the lessons or themes and life patterns that surround your current situation can free you from where you are. This enables you to move on so that you don't keep repeating a particular life pattern. See every experience as a stepping stone to your ultimate outcome. View every experience, whether good or bad, as a teacher.

Once you get the message, the point of a particular situation that keeps occurring and recurring, Life moves you on. Making the most of where you are right now helps to magnetize bigger and better opportunities.

Mike Dooley, creator of *Notes from the Universe*, explains that we need to master what is before us, master our current circumstances and deal with what is on our plate now. He says that where you are now is your "sacred launch pad" and the fastest way to free yourself from what you don't like is to get on top of it.

Money Love

To attract financial abundance, we need to adjust our relationship with money and align our habits so that they are congruent with the creation and accumulation of wealth.

We need to eliminate our ambivalence towards money and wealth.

Do you equate abundance with self-indulgence?

Do you choose to see money as an instrument of greed, an agent of stress, a means of control, or a method of slavery?

Or do you choose to view money as a tool that empowers us, gives us food, shelter, possessions, education and resources?

We also have to detach our emotional behaviour from our activities with money. One example of this kind of emotional behaviour is if we are prone to purchasing gadgets and clothes etc. in order to cheer ourselves up when we are feeling down. It is similar to emotional behaviour that is attached to food (like binge eating for comfort).

We have five physical senses and in Chapter Ten, we explored our corresponding inner subjective senses. But one sense that we haven't talked about much is the importance of basic common sense. Dream big, but don't throw logic out of the window.

This means taking into account the usual practical principles, such as making sure that your day-to-day habits are in alignment with your plans for wealth, for example, by reducing or eliminating the use of credit cards as well as saving as much as you can from what you earn.

Nowadays human beings have an increased lifespan and in many cultures, people are expected to live well past the age of 80. Spontaneous spending, impulse buying, immediate consumption and short-term consumerism are therefore not conducive to building long term wealth. We need to adjust our spending habits so that they take into account the possibility of a long-term future.

"If I were a rich man..."

At a social and cultural level, our collective psychology is at odds with consistent wealth creation therefore many of us need to reprogram and recondition ourselves.

Detach yourself from the collective social perception of reality (as discussed in Chapter Eight). Don't be swayed by what you are being told about the economy, recession, Depression, national debt and other financial obstacles. That may be the reality of the social situation and it may be a national or global reality. But it doesn't have to be *your* personal individual fate. There are plenty of people who thrive financially no matter how badly the economy is behaving.

Many view a lottery win as being the easiest path to financial abundance.

People are always talking about all the wonderful things they would do and contribute if they won the lottery. But the weekly/hourly/monthly wage combined with the weekly purchase of a lottery ticket is not the road to riches for most. Many people who do hit the jackpot and win the lottery end up losing all their winnings in a short space of time because they do not have an abundance mentality.

187

A lady, who worked as a cleaner, won over a million pounds in one of the National Lottery draws. Within twelve months, she had spent all her money and was working for a different organisation as a new cleaner.

We each have a "financial boundary" or our own internal glass ceiling and even if fortune smiles upon us, sometimes we are not smiling upon ourselves. Our attitudes and habits are stronger than the impact of fate. In fact, our attitudes and habits determine our fate.

There are people who earn six figure salaries but who are still struggling to make ends meet and who never seem to have enough to spend, whereas other people who earn much less money are thriving and feeling profitable and successful. The difference between these two categories of people is attitude. The latter group of people possess the abundance mindset.

Entrepreneurial leader, Ali Brown, says that no amount of money can make you feel economically safe. Only a mindset of abundance can empower you enough to make you feel financially free because you know that if you lose all your money through life circumstances, you will almost instantly be able to earn that money back with your abundant attitude.

Comparing yourself with those you perceive as being more successful can lead to defeatist thinking, pessimism, depression and despair.

Criticising those who already have what you would like to have repels it from your life – because your mind will associate their material advantages with the kind of people that they are. If they are people that you find objectionable, your mind will link attracting wealth with obnoxious behaviour.

One shortcut to manifestation is to bless those who already have what you aspire to have and to affirm to yourself, "This nearly is mine."

It is part of Huna wisdom and philosophy to bless those who already have what you would like to have. This should be an abundance practice, even if you feel that the people enjoying abundance don't deserve it and even if you don't approve of how they are using their privileges. When you come into your riches, you already know that you will make different, more positive and empowering choices.

Don't be one of the crabs in the bucket pulling other people down and don't be a dog in the manger that discourages people from getting what you think you don't want.

Envy (as opposed to the dark poisonous emotions of jealousy) can be a powerful positive tool indicating to you what you truly desire, the qualities you would like to emulate and the benefits that you would like to enjoy.

Resenting other people's good is a massive block to manifestation, wealth and abundance.

There is an amusing anecdote in T. Harv Ecker's book *Secrets of the Millionaire Mind*. He was watching the Hollywood actress Halle Berry in an interview on TV talking about securing one of the highest fees for her work. She said that she pursued this fee on behalf of all the women in her industry. He initially felt a wave of scepticism at her motives.

But T. Harv Ecker is one of the masters of creating financial abundance and teaching others how to attract it. So when he noticed his wave of negativity towards Miss Berry's earning power, he immediately decided to cancel it out by shouting at the TV screen, "Way to go, Halle! You go, girl! You deserve it! You should have asked for more! Etc!"

Happy are the poor

You also have to BELIEVE that you DESERVE wealth and abundance and good times...or else...

If you feel unworthy or like a bad person or undeserving in anyway, then self-forgiveness and releasing yourself from past mistakes and painful memories will help to diminish the delays and blocks to the accomplishment of your goals. (You can apply the Emotional Stress Release technique as described in Chapter Eight to any self-forgiveness issues and challenges.)

Remember that genuinely "bad" people don't usually feel undeserving or unworthy (at least not consciously). They don't usually beat themselves up. In fact, they go the other way and can usually justify or rationalise their behaviour to themselves. Though they may be self-absorbed, they may not be self-aware, whereas people who are overly self-critical about their perceived flaws and failings are usually more guilty of perfectionism than any great crime or misdemeanour.

Organised religion may play a large part here. If your religion suggests or implies that wealth is sinful and that poor people are virtuous – (or if this doctrine was part of your upbringing)– you may unconsciously block or close down opportunities for wealth because at some level, you equate abundance with indulgence or sin.

You may also believe at some level that you are supposed to suffer during your lifetime on Earth and that the good times will come only in the Hereafter.

If this is your belief, conscious or unconscious, or if it was once your belief at some stage in your life, somewhere inside of yourself, you may feel that you are supposed to be postponing the good times until after you die and that you are not supposed to be happy right now. (That is, if you equate money with good times or with happiness)

During childhood, one biblical story had a much bigger impact on my financial mentality than I realised. (In fact, it was only when I was writing this chapter that I realised this.) It was the story of a good but very rich man who wanted to become a disciple of Jesus. Because he was already a good man, Jesus said the only thing left for him to do in order to become his disciple was to give away all his money and possessions. The man was too attached to his affluent lifestyle to do this and went away sadly.

Then Jesus said, *"It is easier for a camel to go through the eye of a needle than for a rich man to enter heaven."* Even though he did add, "But all things are possible with God", the camel and needle thing seems to have stuck with me unconsciously only to be unearthed decades later when thinking about what I was going to include in this chapter.

Money doesn't equal good times or bad times or happiness or sin. People can do great things with and because of money.

190

Other people can create evil with and because of money. Money is just a symbol of how financially rich or deprived you are. It is not good or bad in itself.

The Mythology of Money

As we have already discussed, the way that you show up and act in the world is always consistent with your deepest self-image – and this includes the financial results that you get.

If you don't recognise that your beliefs about money are opinions and not facts, this can also shut down your options and freeze your financial situation.

Similar to our relationship with food or our self-image, during our formative years, we pick up messages, impressions and ideas about money without realising it. We absorb it unconsciously and internalise it.

Your personal story or mythology about money will reflect and parallel your story, mythology and history about other aspects of your life such as your career or relationships and your overall worldview ("Life sucks!" or "This world is a vale of tears" or "Life is a miracle." Or "Every day presents a new opportunity.")

Your identity affects how you see and relate to money so who you think you are will also reflect your situation with money.

Changing the image in the internal mirror and your beliefs will transform your relationship with money – which for the most part has been formed unconsciously. See Chapter Seven for a review about changing the image in your internal mirror.

You can also reflect upon the attitudes of your parents/guardians, teachers and peers' towards money when you were growing up and examine which, if any, of their attitudes, beliefs and behaviours you have adopted as your own.

The Seven Qualities of Abundance

Financial wealth is only one facet of abundance. Most of us would like to achieve a sense of satisfaction and fulfilment that doesn't only come from the amount of money that is sitting in our bank account.

There are seven essential qualities that we can develop in order to attract material, psychological and spiritual abundance.

1.   Generosity

As well as visualising what you would like to get out of life, **visualise what you want to give back** and what you want to contribute. As High Performance Coach, Brendon Burchard often teaches, "Give and you shall receive." This is also the central premise of the book *The Go-Giver* by authors Bob Burg and John David Mann.

Generosity does not necessarily mean giving money to charity. You can be generous with your time, generous with the energy you give to others and generous with your thoughts towards other people. Cultivating a practice of wishing other people well can actually have the effect of uplifting you.

Prosperity teacher and minister, Catherine Ponder calls this the "law of increase". Whatever you dish out to the world can come back to you multiplied. Conversely, the practice of dwelling on negativity, criticising and belittling others, she calls "the law of decrease".

One of the biggest blocks to manifestation is constant complaining. I don't mean constructive complaints when we have a right to get our voice heard, such as when you've received poor service from a provider, or restaurant or company.

By constant complaining, I mean, moaning and bitching about everyday things that can't be helped (such as the weather, public transport, the economy, your annoying colleagues, celebrities, political scandals and so on). This type of moaning increases stress and negativity and slows down or blocks the manifestation process. Holding grudges is another great manifestation blocker and abundance eater.

The unfortunate thing is that many of us love to complain. We even build great bonds over our shared mishaps. Many friendships thrive over a shared meal whose ingredients include blame, resentment or victimhood.

As Abraham Lincoln and Pollyanna/Hayley Mills both said, "If you look for the bad in mankind expecting to find it, you surely will."

Get into the habit of talking in terms of your positive experiences, your successes and what is going well for you (without sounding as if you're bragging, of course).

If your energy is always focused on what is going wrong, you will only attract more of it. It never rains, but it pours, people say, when they are experiencing a run of "bad luck".

What you see affects your reality. In the field of quantum physics, the behaviour of subatomic particles changes according to the perspective of the person that is observing the particles. The way in which the particles are observed determines what they become. What takes place on this tiny microscopic level also takes place at a macroscopic level as well.

Generosity with your time, energy and thoughts will be reflected back to you through the Grand Mirror of the Universe and you will get back more than you give out, if you don't give to get, but give authentically because you really want to.

There is also a place for generosity with money.

Many teachers of success, prosperity-thinking and finance espouse the values of tithing. Tithe means tenth. Ten was considered a spiritual or "magical" number of increase in ancient times. Tithing was practised by many of the wealthy ancient civilisations such as the Egyptians, Babylonians, Greeks, Persians, Chinese or Arabians.

Many cultures continue the practice of tithing in the present day. Strictly speaking, tithing is not the same as donating to charity. It involves giving a tenth of everything you earn every month to one particular organization that provides you with emotional or spiritual inspiration. Some people give a tenth of their net income. Others give a tenth of their gross income.

For many people, the particular organisation that they give a tenth of their income to may be a religious institution. For others, it may be given to a place that once provided them with healing, such as a hospital. Others who have no spiritual allegiances may prefer to give a tenth of their income to a humanitarian organisation or a place of learning that has special meaning for them.

People have reported amazing results, not just in monetary terms but in other directions, when they give a tenth of everything they earn to one particular organisation over a significant period of time.

2.   Generative

The second quality of abundance is to be generative. You will notice that the words 'generous' and 'generative' have the same root.

To be generative is to be productive – it is the life-giving principle. When we are being generative, we are modelling Nature. We are co-creating with Life itself and tuning in to that aspect of life that is creative, expansive and abundant.

When we are generative, we have an endless reserve of energy. We are able to uplift people with our attention, our presence, our words or with a smile.

To be generative is to be creative, expansive, unlimited but yet grounded. This corresponds with the Earth element in Traditional Chinese philosophy. Nature or the Earth is fertile and has the capacity to constantly generate and renew life. When left alone and untampered, Nature is prolific and productive.

There is joy in the abundance of Nature. Being in natural beautiful surroundings has the power to feed and uplift the soul.

When we give from a mindset of joy, freedom and expansion, we are adopting the generative principle of abundance.

To cultivate a generative attitude, spend time in beautiful natural surroundings or if this is not possible, collect pictures and photographs of images of plenty that come from Nature. Visit luxuriant environments, art galleries, antique shops and museums. Read biographies about successful people.

When you think in terms of your long-term goal, think of ways that you could potentially expand or increase that idea in the future.

Whatever you plan on earning, double or triple that figure in your mind.

When you are focused on giving and generosity, you shouldn't have a problem feeling guilty about receiving or thinking big.

Expand your consciousness to encompass images, thoughts and ideas of plenty. Develop a no-limits mindset. Allow your imagination to be unlimited.

3.   Gratitude

One of the laws of manifestation is that you need to appreciate where you are now and what you have now – no matter how little it is – in order to be given more. (...anyone who has, will be given more; anyone who has not, will be deprived even of what he has." Mark 4:25)

One of the best ways to speed up the manifestation of a goal, project or dream is to cultivate a general overall attitude of gratitude towards life. The more you appreciate what you already have, the more good fortune will come your way and the faster it will come.

Gratitude breeds synchronicity and happiness. And the bonus is that it really does make you feel better – especially when you have had a really bad day.

The Practice of Gratitude

Cultivating gratitude makes you feel good and also has a positive impact on your health by reducing stress. (Stress, as you know, reduces the effectiveness of the immune system, leaving you vulnerable to all kinds of illnesses or chronic diseases).

There are many levels of practising gratitude and appreciation. Here are five examples which you may like to practise. The list starts with the simplest practice and progresses toward the most challenging or time-consuming practices.

Level One

As the old song says, "Count your blessings, name them one by one."

You can mentally think of all the things you are grateful for as you drift off to sleep every night.

Level Two

In her book *Simple Abundance,* Sarah Ban Breathnach speaks about keeping a gratitude journal where you list five things that you are grateful for each day. Sometimes you will list things that are specific to that day. But when you've had one of those days from hell and can think of nothing good that happened, you can list what you are generally grateful for in life – like having a home, food or family.

Level Three

Instead of making a simple short list in your gratitude journal, you could write for fifteen minutes a day about exactly what it is you are grateful for and why.

Level Four

Darren Hardy describes the practice of choosing something in your life that is causing you frustration and writing about why you are grateful for that situation for 21 days. He says that when you change the way you look at something, how you perceive that thing changes.

Level Five

Feminine Power teacher, Katherine Woodward-Thomas advocates a daily practice of writing five full pages of prose describing all the things that you are grateful about for thirty days. This practice involves not only being grateful for the good things in your life but finding something positive to write about the challenges, setbacks and ordeals you may be going through. It is the art of appreciating things exactly the way that they are now before you can move on. She says that the more attention you give to lack, the more of it you generate whereas the more you focus on what you have, the more joy you feel and consequently the more you receive from the people around you, Nature and the Universe.

4. **Optimism**

Optimism is the fourth quality of abundance. Martin Seligman, considered to be one of the founders of positive psychology has written a book called *Learned Optimism*. Learned optimism is one of the antidotes to learned helplessness.

When thinking about optimism, I am reminded of a scene in the hilarious film *Clockwise* when the headmaster (played by John Cleese) says with anguish, "It's not the despair, it's the *hope."*

Many of us fear disappointment so we do not like to hope for the best because failure is all the more crushing and devastating to deal with when it is unexpected.

Some scientists view optimism as the opposite of realism. Some neuroscientists even interpret optimism as a brain defect rather than as a positive characteristic.

Poor old Pollyanna tends to get a bad rap but her simple philosophy of "being glad" and adopting an optimistic outlook is one of the three basic stepping stones to leading a life that is filled with abundance. (The other two basics are enthusiasm and gratitude).

Optimism involves not only being positive about the future but about the past as well and being able to see the positive aspect or constructive meaning in even the most painful memories.

Being optimistic about the past means choosing to view the challenges that you have survived as something that made you stronger rather than as reasons that explain why you haven't already achieved what you wanted to achieve or building a case for why you aren't yet where you think you ought to be.

Optimism is the belief that Life is on your side, that Life is conspiring to bring about your greater happiness and that the Universe is not out to get you but to support you.

5.   Enthusiasm

There are many levels of depression – mild, severe, clinical and these may include types of depression that may be caused by hormonal or chemical imbalances.

However when I refer to depression in this context, I am talking about the basic kind of every day depression that is not due to a long-term medical or clinical condition and that anyone can suffer with from time to time.

At the most basic level, when we are depressed, it tends to mean that we have little hope, enthusiasm or excitement for the future. We feel disconnected from ourselves, disconnected from others and disconnected from Life or a Spiritual Source.

Generating a feeling of enthusiasm about life (because of or in spite of our circumstances) can help to combat that quiet background feeling of despair and malaise that can gnaw away at us in our daily life.

The word 'enthusiasm' comes from the Greek and can be literally translated as "filled with God" or "God within".

Another way to define the word 'enthusiasm' is "full of life" or "full of vital energy". There is a sense of excitement that propels us from day to day no matter what we are doing and no matter how humdrum our existence may seem.

According to High Performance teacher, Brendon Burchard, the three questions to keep in mind when you want to keep refreshed, enthusiastic and full of zeal about your life so that you have the energy to manifest your goal is:

What am I grateful for that happened yesterday?
What can I do for myself today to make it special?
What am I excited about for tomorrow?

This kind of thinking encompasses past, present and future.

It is important to consciously cultivate good memories and focus on past happy experiences when looking backwards because your mental Storehouse of Knowledge interprets all new information, new people and new experiences through the lens of past association.

Another way to generate enthusiasm is to practise the One Minute Joy exercise as described in Jean Houston's book *A Passion for the Possible*.

For this exercise, you may need to use an egg timer, an alarm or the timer on your mobile phone. Choose a joyful memory or experience from your past. Focus on it for one full minute recalling images, words, sounds, tastes, emotions and smells. When the minute is up, you will feel energised, joyful and enthusiastic.

6.   Passion

Passion is the sixth quality of abundance.

Passion is born out of purpose. Purpose is born out of *why* you are doing what you are doing and why it is important to you. This keeps you driven and "on purpose".

This is why we focused on the reasons behind why you want to accomplish your goal at the start of this book.

Finding something to be passionate about and being able to do it at any level (big or small) shakes us out of that feeling that we are leading a life of "quiet desperation", grey mediocrity and humdrum routine.

Passion means doing something or going after something for the love of it, and not because you want to prove to yourself, or to other people, that you are good enough, worthy enough or talented enough.

Some people unconsciously postpone happiness until they achieve what they set out to achieve.

But passion is the art of enjoying the journey instead of waiting until you reach the destination.

In the first chapter, I talked about the Martin Luther King quote: "A man who hasn't found something he is willing to die for is not fit to live."

If we don't interpret this statement in its most literal sense, it could mean, if you don't have anything in your life that you feel strongly about, you won't be able to get the most out of the short time that you spend here.

7.   Receptive

So you've been generous with your time and energy. You send people silent blessings, thoughts of love and wish them well. You've stopped complaining. You never criticise people or gossip.

You read books about inspiring people and take long walks in nature. You're optimistic about the past. You're enthusiastic and excited about everything you do. You are practising the five levels of the gratitude and you are enjoying the journey.

And then good things start happening, people offer you compliments and gifts and opportunities and presents – and you turn them all down. You feel awkward about charging high fees for your services. You are unable to receive and you feel unworthy, undeserving or that it would be too greedy to accept all the good things that are coming your way. The abundance stops. Good things stop happening or stall. You are confused.

What's gone wrong? What have you missed?

You've missed out the seventh quality of abundance.

The seventh principle is receptivity. This means giving yourself permission to receive the good things in life. You do not question whether you are worthy enough or deserving of other people's praise, compliments, gifts, good wishes and offers of help. You receive all good things that come your way with acceptance and gratitude.

Be willing to receive compliments and presents with a "thank you". Do not respond to a remark of appreciation with a casual, "Oh, it was nothing" and don't dismiss their compliments ("What, this old thing?").

Accepting gifts from others with enthusiasm and pleasure is a way of giving back to them. In order for someone to be generous, there has to be someone who is willing to accept generosity. It is part of the energy exchange cycle. So receive and you will give.

Accepting gifts with joy and gratitude is a way of manifesting more abundance. The Universe will send you more because you have demonstrated that you are ready to receive.

These seven qualities of abundance tie up and summarise everything that has been discussed and explored in this book.

Focusing on these seven principles of abundance (together with the seven principles of success) will move you upward into greater levels of achievement and fulfilment, enabling you to manifest things that you never knew you wanted, in ways that you never knew existed and in ways that you never before believed were possible.

Acknowledgements

Special thanks to the following people whose work has informed, inspired and laid the foundations for this system of Manifestation Psychology:

Roberto Assagioli
Sarah Ban Breathnach
Michael Bernard Beckwith
Nathaniel Branden
Brendon Burchard
Deepak Chopra
Lou D'Alo
Mike Dooley
Emma Eker
T. Harv Eker
Darren Hardy
Jean Houston
Carl Jung
Lester Levensen
Eben Pagan
Will Parfitt
Catherine Ponder
Jane Roberts
Jose Silva
Brian Tracy
PaTrisha Anne Todd
Iyanla Vanzant
Ken Wilber
Katherine Woodward-Thomas
Claire Zammit

Last but not least, I would also like to thank Vilma for proofreading this book.

For more information about manifestation psychology, visit: http://www.manifestationpsychology.com

3673702R00120

Printed in Great Britain
by Amazon.co.uk, Ltd.,
Marston Gate.